S0-BPI-628

THE BIBLIOGRAPHY OF CONTEMPORARY AMERICAN POETRY, 1945–1985: AN ANNOTATED CHECKLIST

LITERARY BIBLIOGRAPHIES
FROM MECKLER PUBLISHING

Series Editor: Stuart Wright

Walker Percy: A Bibliography: 1930–1984
by Stuart Wright
ISBN 0-88736-046-7 CIP 1986

The Bibliography of Contemporary American Poetry, 1945–1985: An Annotated Checklist
by William McPheron
ISBN 0-88736-054-8 CIP 1986

John Ciardi: A Descriptive Bibliography
by Charles C. Lovett and Stephanie B. Lovett
ISBN 0-88736-056-4 CIP *forthcoming*

William Goyen: A Descriptive Bibliography
by Stuart Wright
ISBN 0-88736-057-2 CIP *forthcoming*

Robinson Crusoe: An Annotated Checklist of English Language Editions, 1719–1985
by Robert W. Lovett
ISBN 0-88736-058-0 CIP *forthcoming*

Donald Davie: A Descriptive Bibliography
by Stuart Wright
ISBN 0-88736-059-9 CIP- *forthcoming*

Harry Crews: A Descriptive Bibliography
by Michael Hargraves
ISBN 0-88736-060-2 CIP *forthcoming*

THE BIBLIOGRAPHY OF CONTEMPORARY AMERICAN POETRY, 1945–1985: AN ANNOTATED CHECKLIST

PS
323.5
.M36x
1986
West

WILLIAM MCPHERON

MECKLER PUBLISHING

ASU WEST LIBRARY

Library of Congress Cataloging in Publication Data

McPheron, William.
  The bibliography of contemporary American poetry,
1945–1985.

  Bibliography: p.
  1. American poetry—20th century—Bibliography.
I. Title.
Z1231.P7M37   1986   [PS323.5]   016.811'54   85-29850
ISBN 0-88736-054-8

Copyright © 1986 by Meckler Publishing

All rights reserved. No part of this publication may be reproduced
in any form by any means without prior permission in writing
from the publisher, except by a reviewer who may quote brief
passages in review.

Meckler Publishing, 11 Ferry Lane West, Westport, CT 06880
Meckler Publishing, 3 Henrietta Street, London WC2E 8LU, UK

Printed and bound in the United States of America

Contents

PREFACE

This checklist records and briefly characterizes bibliographical studies of contemporary American poets. Its purpose is double: to indicate the historical evolution as well as the present state of the field and to highlight those poets in need of additional, or original bibliographical research.

The section on multi-author sources is organized alphabetically by compiler, editor, or title and notes only works whose intent is to provide significant coverage of individual poets and of the small presses that have published so much of their work. Excluded are the indexes and serial bibliographies—both general and specialized—which treat the materials of contemporary verse but do not feature single-author or individual press compilations.

The section for specific writers concentrates on poets whose reputations have been established since 1945. This scope deliberately extends to some poets, such as Randall Jarrell, Robert Lowell, Theodore Roethke, and Kenneth Rexroth, whose first books appeared in the early 1940s but whose full recognition was not achieved until after the end of World War II. Also included are two Objectivists, George Oppen, and

Louis Zukofsky, who were active in the 1930s but went unknown and virtually unpublished until the 1950s and 1960s. Excluded are writers whose poetry is incidental to their fiction, contributing insignificantly to their literary careers.

Entries under the poets in the single-author section are arranged chronologically, then alphabetically by compiler within the year. Only bibliographically serious accounts are recorded. Highly selective checklists routinely appearing in critical monographs or printed in issues of journals specially devoted to a poet have been excluded, except in a few cases where no other coverage is available. Bibliographies appended to unpublished doctoral dissertations and masters theses have also been excluded, but dissertations and theses that are full-scale bibliographical studies have been noted. Within these limits, the checklist is intended to be complete, but lapses are inevitable. Additions and corrections are welcome.

An earlier version of the introduction that follows was presented as part of the program, "Literary Bibliographies: Defining Standards for Their Creation and Evaluation," held at the convention of the Modern Language Association of America in December 1983 and chaired by Elaine A. Franco of the University of Nebraska, Lincoln. There are also other debts it is a pleasure to acknowledge. Stuart Wright's editorial hand stayed misjudged inclusions and inadvertent omissions. Robert J. Bertholf generously shared his own superb knowledge of both contemporary literature and bibliography. And most literally indispensable was Marcie Peperone's secretarial genius.

State University of New York at Buffalo   William McPheron
                                                      November 1985

INTRODUCTION

In the decades immediately following World War II, American poetry
entered upon an unusually energetic, prolific, and radically pluralistic
period. A convenient index of these extraordinary years is provided by
four benchmark anthologies issued between 1957 and 1965: New Poets of
England and America, compiled by Donald Hall, Robert Pack, and Louis
Simpson (New York: Meridian, 1957), its sequel, New Poets of England
and America: A Second Selection, chosen by Hall and Pack
(Cleveland: Meridian/World Publishing, 1962), The New American Poetry:
1945-1960, organized by Donald M. Allen (New York: Grove, 1960), and
finally, the aptly titled A Controversy of Poets: An Anthology of
Contemporary American Poetry, gathered by Paris Leary and Robert Kelly
(Garden City, N.Y.: Anchor/Doubleday, 1965). Each collection intended
to feature the new generation's most significant poets and is notable
for the sheer number of writers featured and for the singular lack of
agreement among them. Fifty-four different American poets, all under
forty, appear in the two versions of New Poets of England and America,
while The New American Poetry, selecting largely from the same age group,
offers the work of forty-four--only one of which, surprisingly, is

included in either of the other anthologies. A Controversy of Poets, published slightly later, is by contrast self-consciously eclectic; but its choices, while suggesting the outlines of a consensus, principally act to extend even further the boundaries of conflicting judgment. For, of its fifty-nine poets, fully twenty-five are absent from the three earlier volumes. In short, four major collections, published within eight years of each other, propose no less than 122 different writers as the leading representatives of contemporary American verse.

Equally remarkable is that this sudden emergence into visibility of new talent continues unabated with the present generation. The great number and wide variety of these younger voices are once again effectively indexed by anthologies. Comparison of such recent collections as Roger Gaess's Leaving the Bough: 50 American Poets of the 80s (New York: International Publishers, 1982), William Heyen's The Generation of 2000: Contemporary American Poets (Princeton, N.J.: Ontario Review Press, 1984), and the Morrow Anthology of Younger American Poets (New York: Morrow, 1985) compiled by Dave Smith and David Bottoms enforces the point that contemporary American poetry remains in a state of explosive growth. This condition was made possible and continues to be sustained by several basic changes in the circumstances of poetry in the postwar era, each of which had important bibliographic consequences. First, the modernist strategy of self-publication through little magazines and small presses has been dramatically extended by the introduction of inexpensive forms of reproduction. Though the letterpress tradition of quality alternative publishing continues to flourish, more importantly, the use of multilith copiers, mimeograph machines, and photo-offset printing has produced a quantum leap in the total output of contemporary literature—most of it in small editions with very limited distribution. Second, during this period, creative writing programs in English departments proliferated throughout the country. Such active training and encouragement of young poets has had the direct effect of multiplying the number of academically sponsored journals devoted to printing their work and also has indirectly brought university presses into the business of publishing contemporary poetry. Though more conventional in content and format than their avant-garde counterparts, these publications, particularly the magazines, are often produced in short runs and generally ignored by existing literary indexes. Also associated with campus communities, but serving anti-academic poets as well, has been a third set of new tools for achieving visibility: public poetry readings, the related phenomena of poetry conferences, and the formal interviews that frequently attended these events have become important avenues for disseminating current work. The presence of the portable, battery-powered tape recorder allows the routine taping of these sessions, thereby creating a large body of permanent documents central to the understanding of postmodern verse. But most of these artifacts remain largely undistributed, untranscribed, and uncataloged.

These fundamental changes, combined with such allied developments as the growing popularity of broadsides, poem-cards, and other fugitive formats, have resulted in a bibliographic nightmare that threatens to render systematic study of new American poetry increasingly difficult. But scholars have responded to the challenge, and though no match for the poets' vitality, they have made remarkable progress. For instance, of the 122 poets featured in the above mentioned pioneering anthologies, more than one in three has now been the subject of serious bibliographic attention. Included in this figure are 43 separately published, book-length studies and almost half again that number of individual articles;

not counted are the limited but still useful treatments in such multi-author reference tools as <u>Contemporary Poets</u> and <u>First Printings of American Authors</u>, or the highly selective lists conventionally appended to critical monographs. But beyond this growing body of work, perhaps a more certain sign that the bibliography of contemporary American verse is indeed reaching maturity is the field's being haunted by at least two ghosts of non-existent bibliographies, whose putative presence is nonetheless regularly invoked in the literature.(1)

The push to provide bibliographic access to the revolution occurring in American poetry appropriately began with the small presses and little magazines themselves. Earliest on the scene was Alan Swallow, who was producing his <u>Index to Little Magazines</u> by 1949. More characteristic were publishers accounting for their own authors. City Lights, whose owner, Lawrence Ferlinghetti, had been arrested in 1956 for publishing Allen Ginsberg's <u>Howl and Other Poems</u>, issued a full-length treatment of Ginsberg's work fifteen years later. John Martin inaugurated his Black Sparrow Press with a broadside by Charles Bukowski, the first of nearly forty Bukowski items he has since printed--one of which was a comprehensive bibliography of the writer. And Robert Wilson's Phoenix Bookshop, with close ties to the avant-garde movement generally, has sponsored a series of single-author bibliographies focused largely on Beat and Black Mountain writers. The little magazines have also contributed significantly to bibliographic order. Fred Candelaria's <u>West Coast Review</u>, Michael Cuddihy's <u>Ironwood</u>, and Robert Bertholf's <u>Credences</u>, to name only a few presently active, have regularly featured checklists of poets whose work they have sponsored. The motive behind these efforts by the alternative press has in large measure been collegial concern for the poetry itself, so that concentration has been on recording and describing primary texts. As to the general quality of this work, it is consistently good but seldom definitive.

Typical is the case of Edward Dorn, who in 1973 was the subject of two independent studies, a Phoenix Bookshop descriptive bibliography and an enumerative checklist of items both by and about him in Douglas Calhoun's little magazine, <u>Athanor</u>. Aspiring to completeness, both move across a wide range of print and non-print materials, from wrapper notes to recordings. The descriptions in the first study are modified, abbreviated forms of the model established by Donald Gallup in his frequently imitated <u>A Bibliography of Ezra Pound</u> (London: Rupert Hart-Davis, 1963; 2d ed. 1969; 3rd rev. ed. Charlottesville: Univ. Press of Virginia, 1983). Each study contains items lacking but properly belonging in the other, while both overlook some minor pieces altogether. These lapses are, however, not of major importance, and taken together the volumes furnish a thorough, if peripherally incomplete record of Dorn's career. But such reliability is not always characteristic of the small presses and little magazines. For example, the Ginsberg bibliography from City Lights suffers in both organization and detail from the self-acknowledged amateurism of its compiler, and a James Wright checklist in a 1977 issue of <u>Ironwood</u> is marred by omissions and inaccuracies, which were unnecessary, since three years earlier the <u>Bulletin of Bibliography</u> had covered Wright thoroughly.

These failures are exceptional, but in their indifference to the conventions of academic practice, they represent a problem common to the best alternative press work. This is the refusal to fully articulate bibliographic principles and methods. Black Sparrow's book-length treatment of Louis Zukofsky illustrates this tendency: compiled by the poet's wife and published in a signed, limited edition, the bibliography has no prefatory statement, yet it employs some unorthodox notations that require explanation. Such work clearly springs from personal engagement with the poetry, not serious interest in bibliography itself, and its disregard of academic habits is understandable. But it is no less unfortunate, since both the quality of work itself and responses to a survey of operating policies testify to the alternative press's concern for rigorous bibliographic standards.(2)

Sharing this concern, but at the opposite stylistic pole, are the university presses. Also emphasizing descriptive accounts of primary materials, their work has been in contrast sharply self-conscious about methodology. Basic motives have been twofold: both the academic impulse to advance the discipline of bibliography, and the need of collectors for more detailed information have shaped university press publications. Most evident in the field are the Serif Series of Kent State, the Linton R. Massey Descriptive Bibliographies from Virginia, and the Pittsburgh Series in Bibliography. Though their twentieth-century volumes have concentrated on modernist writers, some entry into the postmodern era has been made, and these contributions have expanded and conventionalized the types of materials treated, so that accounts of dust jacket blurbs, keepsakes, and proof copies are now routine. Representative of progress in this context is the incorporation of unpublished sources in the Serif volume devoted to Robert Creeley: besides recording, the locations and contents of manuscripts, it cross references them to their published counterparts, for which it further provides composition dates derived from the manuscripts. Also notable is a different handling of unpublished documents in the Virginia study of Elizabeth Bishop: here, manuscript letters are used to elucidate the bibliographical history of the books described.

The university presses have also dramatically intensified the level of physical description. Adopting Fredson Bowers' <u>Principles of Bibliographical Description</u> (Princeton, N.J.: Princeton Univ. Press, 1949) as a model and introducing new elements as printing circumstances demanded, these studies employ the most advanced techniques of treating modern books. Here Pittsburgh's volume on John Berryman is exemplary, with its exact presentation of dust jackets and registration of variants between different book appearances of individual poems. Though there are problems with these university press products, they tend to be the defects of their aspirations (see, e.g., Craig Abbott, "Bishop Bibliographed: The New Descriptive Bibliography?" <u>Review</u> 3 (1981): 233-242). The complexity of the standards and breadth of information conveyed is an open invitation to omissions and errors. But with usually greater financial resources and the aggressive commitment of editorial boards to improving the art of bibliography itself, here is the likeliest arena for truly definitive studies.

Also part of the universities and making a minor but noteworthy addition to the bibliographic control of contemporary verse are research libraries, which have regularly published checklists through their bulletins and separate studies under their own imprints. Sometimes these record the institution's holdings, such as the fine catalog of its Zukofsky manuscripts issued by the Humanities Research Center at the University of Texas at Austin. More frequently, the work is occasioned by special collections but not specific to them: recent instances of this pattern are the Joel Oppenheimer and Paul Blackburn checklists published respectively by the libraries of the University of Connecticut-Storrs and the University of California-San Diego, each the repository of the poet's papers. The overall quality of these library studies is high but not definitive, closely comparable to the better publications of the small presses and little magazines.

The other major force providing access to postwar American poetry has been commercial publishers, most prominently Gale, Garland, G. K. Hall, Scarecrow, and Whitson, with the periodicals, the <u>Bulletin of Bibliography</u> and <u>American Book Collector,</u> serving as ready organs for shorter pieces. Their general reference tools, such as the volumes on contemporary poetry in Gale's <u>Information Guide Series</u> and <u>Dictionary of Literary Biography,</u> Kraus-Thomson's <u>Comprehensive Index to English-Language Little Magazines, 1890-1970,</u> and Scarecrow's <u>Index of American Periodical Verse,</u> have helped to raise a bibliographic umbrella over the field. But more important and problematic has been their involvement with single-author studies. For it is here that the exigencies of the marketplace assert themselves most forcefully. This situation is evident from the publishers' responses to a questionnaire, where they collectively ranked the absence of competition as the second most crucial factor in their decision to commit themselves to a single-author bibliography, narrowly ranking it behind the writer's literary prominence. Equally telling is the fact that as a group they assigned more weight to the prospect of competition than to the quality of compilers' proposals or their scholarly credentials. Though this suggests an absolute economic tyranny, half of those publishers responding also stated that the availability of a similar, though inferior quality bibliography was not in itself sufficient reason to refuse issuing another one. This response is verified by such examples as Scarecrow's publishing what proved to be superior volumes on James Dickey and Sylvia Plath and G. K. Hall's similar performance with a

Berryman guide--all issued only a few years after rival treatments had appeared. In each of these instances, the competition consisted, however, of enumerative bibliographies from other commercial publishers.

Where the dictates of profit margins have excluded competition and, indeed, generally prevented quality work altogether, is descriptive bibliography. Commercial ventures here have been relatively few and seldom serious, though recent volumes from Garland devoted to John Ashbery, Frank O'Hara, and Lawrence Ferlinghetti suggest a contrary possibility.

Such exceptions aside, commercial publishers have made their greatest contributions with annotated accounts of secondary materials. These compilations have occasionally been subject to withering contempt, sometimes because reviewers have refused to see the value of this type of work (e.g., Edward Mendelson, "The Rise of the Reference Guide," Times Literary Supplement 27 January 1978: 99), and at other times because the studies failed on their own terms. Instances of embarrassing incompetence have certainly occurred, but more characteristic are the problems identified in Willis J. Buckingham's essay on the G.K. Hall Reference Guides in Literature (Resources for American Literary Study 8 (1978): 200-210). This assessment accurately notes inconsistent principles of inclusion, annotation, and indexing, lapses of editorial attention, and overall confusions of purpose that apply equally to all the commercial publishers of this genre of bibliography.

But the quality of more recent work and the present, clear commitment to outside evaluation promise an increasing level of vigilance. Although only a small minority of the publishers provide written guidelines for their compilers, all except one solicit the judgments of outsider reviewers. Regrettably, the evaluation procedure

itself is not consistently demanding. As a group, only a slim majority
check the accuracy, inclusiveness, and indexing of citations; fortunately
most of the principal publishers fall into the more responsible group.
Though the system now operating hardly matches the rigor of the
university press's editorial boards, it has certainly effected
improvements.

Despite this progress, however, the exasperating failure to define
principles of inclusion unaccountably continues. For example, in the
last several years G. K. Hall has produced a pair of well-executed
studies in contemporary American poetry, one devoted to Robert Lowell,
the other to Elizabeth Bishop and Howard Nemerov. The preface to the
Lowell guide explains precisely its scope, leaving the user in doubt only
at the margins of judgment. In contrast, the Bishop-Nemerov preface does
little more than claim to be "comprehensive," which is belied on the
bibliography's first page. For here, despite the methodological
preface's remarking the interest of Bishop's uncollected juvenalia, the
poet's contributions to her high school literary journal are ignored,
even though these had been fully noted three years earlier in the
Virginia bibliography. The decision to exclude such peripheral materials
was perfectly reasonable, but neglecting to explain it was not. Such
absence of methodological explicitness is now much less common, but its
persistence does more to subvert confidence in the integrity of
commercial press products than occasional oversights and errors.

From a broad view of the achievements in the field as a whole, two
general points emerge. First, bibliography is an omnibus term,
encompassing a variety of different genres, each of which deserves
judgment on its own terms. While descriptive bibliography may be an art
sufficient unto itself, the other forms are unquestionably means serving

larger historical and interpretive ends. To criticize one type of bibliography for its inability to achieve the goals of another is senseless and discourages the less than complete studies that serve as the field's pioneers. What is more crucial in this regard is definition of the purpose, technique, and limits of each genre and frank recognition of their differing orders of legitimacy. Second, bibliography is a process, its published products being momentary crystallizations of an open-ended activity. The best work always announces its provisional nature and anticipates its revised and corrected version. The spirit born of this fact is critical to sustain the essentially shared challenge of accounting for this extraordinary period of American poetry. For while the burden of any particular work rests on the individual compiler, bibliography more than other types of scholarship is a cooperative enterprise requiring the discrete contributions and generosity of many people. Certainly the assertion of standards is equally crucial, but this defense of quality must finally respect the larger fact of bibliographic process.

NOTES

1. Despite numerous references to them, no evidence has been found to confirm the existence of either John Taggart's <u>A Bibliography of Works by Cid Corman</u> (New Rochelle, N.Y.: Elizabeth Press, 1975) or J. M. Edelstein's <u>Robert Lowell: A Checklist</u> (Detroit: Gale, 1973). Katharine McNeil's <u>Gary Snyder: A Bibliography</u> (New York: Phoenix Bookshop), frequently cited as a 1980 volume, finally materialized late in 1983.

2. The mail survey was conducted in the late fall of 1983. The ten-part questionnaire focused both on the methods and factors publishers employ in selecting subjects for author bibliographies and on techniques used to evaluate the compiler's work. Response from small presses and little magazines was not sufficient to report in detail. In contrast, only one commercial publisher of bibliographies failed to reply, and the summary results are presented later in the introduction. University presses were equally cooperative, and their answers underlie the section discussing their contributions to the field.

The Bibliography of
Contemporary American Poetry, 1945–1985:
An Annotated Checklist

MULTI-AUTHOR TOOLS

1. Altieri, Charles F. <u>Modern Poetry</u>. Arlington Heights, Ill.: AHM Publishing, 1979.

   For the major contemporary poets provides selective coverage of primary and secondary sources. Focuses on basic editions of writers' works and records only the most significant criticism.

2. Bruccoli, Matthew J., ed. <u>First Printings of American Authors: Contributions Toward Descriptive Checklists</u>. Detroit: Gale, 1977-1979.

   Lists first editions of separately published works by, or with substantial contributions from, the authors treated. Not descriptive but features facsimile reproductions of some title pages. Numerous contemporary poets included, with coverage occasionally extending to broadsides and major ephemerae.

3. Charters, Ann, ed. <u>The Beats: Literary Bohemians in Postwar America</u>. Vol. 16, Pts. 1-2 of <u>Dictionary of Literary Biography</u>. Detroit: Gale, 1983.

   Provides an introductory bibliography of primary (including

non-print) and secondary materials for each writer treated. Both separately published works and selected periodical appearances by authors are noted. The term "Beats" is construed liberally, so that a wide range of avant-garde poets are included.

4. Contemporary Authors. Detroit: Gale, 1962 - .
    Furnishes checklists of primary works for a very broad range of currently practicing writers. Particularly valuable for minor, or newly emerging, poets not treated elsewhere.

5. Cook, Ralph T. The City Lights Pocket Poets Series: A Descriptive Bibliography. La Jolla, Calif.: Laurence McGilvery; San Diego, Calif.: Atticus Books, 1982.
    Furnishes fully descriptive coverage, supplemented by photographs of covers, for Lawrence Ferlinghetti's series of small format collections of avant-garde poets that were issued by his City Lights Books from 1955 to 1982. Poets represented include the major figures of the Beat, Black Mountain, and New York schools of the postwar period.

6. Cooney, Seamus. A Checklist of the First One Hundred Publications of the Black Sparrow Press. Los Angeles: Black Sparrow Press, 1971.
    This briefly descriptive account of books produced by John Martin's press from 1966 into 1971 is superseded by Item 19.

7. Davis, Lloyd, and Robert Irwin. Contemporary American Poetry: A Checklist. Metuchen, N.J.: Scarecrow, 1975.

Lists only books of poems published by writers active since 1945. Other works by authors treated, whether in different genres or formats, are excluded. Coverage extends through 1973. Useful for minor poets.

8.   Edelstein, J. M.   A Jargon Society Checklist 1951-1979.   [Highlands, N.C.:   Jargon Society], 1979.

An enumerative treatment, with annotations, of the first ninety-two volumes published and planned by Jonathan Williams' press, including work by Charles Olson, Robert Creeley, Joel Oppenheimer, and Paul Metcalf as well as Williams' own poetry.

9. Fox, Hugh.   An Analytical Checklist of Books from Something Else Press.   Paradise, Calif.: Dustbooks, 1974.   Issued as Small Press Review   6.1 (March 1974).

This chronological catalog of publications from Dick Higgins' press includes books, pamphlets, and posters.   Enumerative treatment is supplemented by extensive content notes for works by such writers as Jackson Mac Low and Bern Porter as well as Higgins' own writings.   See also Item 10.

10.   Frank, Peter.   Something Else Press: An Annotated Bibliography. New Paltz, N.Y.:   McPherson & Company, 1983.

Supplemented by photographs of covers, this enumerative treatment of books and pamphlets published from 1964 to 1974 by Dick Higgins' press annotates each entry with both content and bibliographical information.   Largely supersedes Item 9.

11. French, William P., Michael J. Fabre, Amritjit Singh, and Geneviève
        E. Fabre. <u>Afro-American Poetry and Drama, 1760-1975: A Guide
        to Information Sources</u>. Detroit: Gale, 1979.
        Contains section on Afro-American poets practicing in the
        period 1946-1975. Lists books and pamphlets by writers and
        commentary on them. Erratic coverage but valuable for minor
        figures.

12. Gingerich, Martin E. <u>Contemporary Poetry in America and England
        1950-1975: A Guide to Information Sources</u>. Detroit: Gale,
        1983.
        Bulk of volume given to checklists of printed materials by and
        about individual poets. Primary coverage restricted to books
        of poetry, excluding works in other genres and formats. Record
        of secondary references is selective but usefully annotated.
        Coverage extends to 1978, with some later items.

13. Greiner, Donald J., ed. <u>American Poets Since World War II</u>. Vol. 5,
        Pts. 1-2 of <u>Dictionary of Literary Biography</u>. Detroit: Gale,
        1980.
        Lists printed sources by and about important American poets who
        published no more than one volume before 1945. Primary
        coverage includes separately issued books and major
        contributions to periodicals. Secondary references highly
        selective.

14. Hamady, Walter. <u>Two Decades of Hamady and The Perishable Press
        Limited</u>. Mt. Horeb, Wis.: Perishable Press, 1984.
        Hamady's high-quality press has printed the writing of such

poets as Paul Blackburn, Robert Creeley, Joel Oppenheimer, William Stafford, and Diane Wakoski. The descriptive checklist of the press's work from 1964 into 1984 is supplemented by anecdotal accounts of each volume's production as well as by frequent photographs.

15. Harris, Trudier, and Thadious M. Davis. <u>Afro-American Poets Since 1955</u>. Vol. 41 of <u>Dictionary of Literary Biography</u>. Detroit: Gale, 1985.

Emphasizing the younger generation of Afro-American poets whose work was first published in the 1950s and 1960s, this bio-critical dictionary also furnishes a selective but very useful list of both primary and secondary materials for each writer treated. Major periodical appearances not otherwise included in collective books and some non-print items are routinely cited.

16. [Johnston, Alastair]. <u>A Bibliography of the Auerhahn Press & its Successor Dave Haselwood Books</u>. Berkeley: Poltroon Press, 1976.

A descriptive census of books and broadsides produced in San Francisco by Dave Haselwood under the Auerhahn, Haselwood, Batman Gallery, and Oyez imprints from 1958 to 1970. Preceding the checklist is an engaging account of Haselwood's connections with the avant-garde poets whose work he published, including such Beats as Michael McClure and Philip Whalen as well as Black Mountain writers like Charles Olson and John Wieners.

17.   _____.   A Bibliography of the White Rabbit Press.   Berkeley:
      Poltroon Press in association with Anacapa Books, 1985.
      Established at Jack Spicer´s urging in 1957, Joe Dunn´s small
      press published the work of Spicer´s San Francisco circle and
      associated poets, including Helen Adam, Robin Blaser, Robert
      Duncan, and Charles Olson. Providing thorough descriptive
      coverage of books, pamphlets, and ephemerae, the bibliography
      proper is preceded by a useful history of the press.

18.   Lepper, Gary M.   A Bibliographical Introduction to Seventy-Five
      Modern American Authors.   Berkeley: Serendipity Books, 1976.
      Devoted to writers who have achieved prominence since 1945.
      Each checklist includes separately published books, fugitive
      matter (including broadsides, postcards, and other ephemerae),
      and translations, briefly describing for each item its first
      printing and noting any bibliographically significant
      subsequent printings. Edited books, non-print materials, and
      periodical appearances excluded.

19.   Morrow, Bradford, and Seamus Cooney.   A Bibliography of the Black
      Sparrow Press 1966-1978.   Santa Barbara, Calif.:   Black
      Sparrow, 1981.
      Comprehensively descriptive catalog of the more than three
      hundred books, pamphlets, and broadsides produced by John
      Martin´s press through 1978. Exhaustive bibliographical
      accounts are supplemented by photographs of all items, which
      include the work of a wide range of avant-garde poets from

various camps, such as Charles Bukowski, Robert Creeley, Robert Kelly, and Diane Wakoski.

20. Nadel, Ira Bruce. <u>Jewish Writers of North America: A Guide to Information Sources</u>. Detroit: Gale, 1981.

Includes a section on American-Jewish poets that concentrates on contemporary figures. For each, it furnishes a checklist of separate publications by the writer and a selected, lightly annotated record of criticism about him.

21. Peich, Michael. <u>The First Ten: A Penmaen Bibliography</u>. Lincoln, Mass.: Penmaen Press, 1978.

Furnishes descriptive treatment of the books, broadsides, and ephemerae published by Michael McCurdy's press during its first decade. Photographic reproductions of title pages and broadsides supplement the descriptions. Penmaen has issued the work of such contemporary poets as Anthony Hecht, William Heyen, and X. J. Kennedy.

22. Reardon, Joan, and Kristine A. Thorsen. <u>Poetry By American Women, 1900-1975: A Bibliography</u>. Metuchen, N.J.: Scarecrow, 1979.

Records separately published volumes of poetry by writers whose major work appeared in the period 1900-1975. All other genres and formats excluded. Principal value is comprehensiveness; numerous minor writers not treated elsewhere are covered here.

23. Rush, Theressa Gunnels, Carol Fairbanks Myers, and Esther Spring Arata. <u>Black American Writers Past and Present: A Biographical and Bibliographical Dictionary</u>. 2 vols. Metuchen, N.J.:

Scarecrow, 1975.

Lists books and some anthology and periodical appearances by the writers treated, along with highly selective accounts of commentary on them. Principal value lies in coverage of minor contemporary figures.

24. Silet, Charles L. P.   "David Kherdian and the Giligia Press." Poet and Critic 9.1 (1975): 39-46.

A history of this Fresno, California press precedes a checklist of its publications, which includes Kherdian's own poetry as well as books related to the Beats.

25. Twayne's United States Author Series. Boston: G. K. Hall, 1961 - .

This monographic series of introductory studies regularly treats contemporary poets.   Each volume concludes with a selective bibliography of primary and secondary sources. Entries for commentary on the writer are well annotated.

26. Vinson, James, ed.   Contemporary Poets. 4th ed.   London: Macmillan; New York: St. Martin's Press [forthcoming, 1985]; 3rd ed., 1980; 2nd ed., 1975; 1st ed., 1970.

Provides basic and generally reliable lists of the separately published books of a very broad range of poets practicing in English. Selective list of secondary sources also furnished.

SINGLE-AUTHOR STUDIES

AMMONS, A. R. (1926 -)

27. Wright, Stuart. <u>A. R. Ammons: A Bibliography 1954-1979</u>. Winston-Salem, N.C.: Wake Forest University, 1980.

Comprehensively treats printed materials by Ammons, including interviews, published comments, and miscellaneous items through 1979. Detailed physical descriptions of separately issued works are supplemented by notes indicating reprintings of individual pieces. Coverage of first book and periodical appearances of poems extends to subsequent publication in collections. Entries for prose accompanied by annotations that summarize the content.

28. _____. "A. R. Ammons: A Bibliographical Checklist." <u>American Book Collector</u> 1.3 (May-June 1980): 32-37.

Focuses exclusively on separately published primary works, with brief descriptions of books by or with contributions from Ammons, into 1980.

ASHBERY, JOHN (1927 -)

29. Kermani, David. John Ashbery: A Comprehensive Bibliography. New
     York: Garland, 1976.

     Provides a thorough account of primary materials (including
     art criticism and artworks) through mid-1975. Treatment is
     fully descriptive, with supplementary notes--often drawing on
     unpublished sources--furnishing important bibliographical
     information. Brief and eccentric secondary section is
     restricted to a selection of references excluded from standard
     indexes.

BARAKA, AMIRI (Jones, LeRoi) (1934 -)

30. Dace, Letitia. LeRoi Jones (Imamu Amiri Baraka): A Checklist of
     Works By and About Him. London: Nether Press, 1971.

     Exhaustive coverage of both primary and secondary materials
     through 1969, with some items from 1970. Treatment of books is
     descriptive, with reviews listed after entry. Writings about
     Baraka are arranged in topical sections, with many very brief
     and inconsequential references included. Significant
     discussions designated by an asterisk but no entries are
     annotated.

31. Hudson, Theodore R. A LeRoi Jones (Amiri Baraka) Bibliography: A
     Keyed Research Guide to Works by LeRoi Jones and to Writing
     about Him and His Works. Washington, D.C.: priv. publ., 1971.

     Both primary and secondary sections arranged alphabetically,
     with all entries coded to indicate genre of piece or topic of

discussion. Limited coverage extends into 1971; useful for its subject analysis. See also Item 33.

32. Shatt, Stanley. "LeRoi Jones: A Checklist of Primary and Secondary Sources." <u>Bulletin of Bibliography and Magazine Notes</u> 28.2 (April–June 1971): 55–57.

Limited coverage, drawn principally from citations in standard indexes. Secondary items are annotated.

33. Hudson, Theodore. "An Imamu Amiri Baraka (LeRoi Jones) Bibliography: A Keyed Guide to Selected Works By and About Him." <u>Black Books Bulletin</u> 2 (Fall 1974): 71–79.

Updates Item 31, bringing coded coverage into 1973.

34. Cohn, Alan M. "Additions to Dace's LeRoi Jones (Imamu Amiri Baraka)." <u>Papers of the Bibliographical Society of America</u> 70.4 (1976): 537–538.

Provides minor additions and corrections to Item 30.

35. Dace, Letitia. "Amiri Baraka (LeRoi Jones)." In <u>Black American Writers: Bibliographical Essays</u>. Ed. M. Thomas Inge, Maurice Duke, and Jackson R. Bryer. Vol. 2. New York: St. Martin's, 1978, 121–178.

Useful evaluative account of bibliographical and critical studies of Baraka into 1976.

36. Sollors, Werner. "Selected Bibliography." In his <u>Amiri Baraka/ LeRoi Jones: The Quest for a "Populist Modernism"</u>. New York: Columbia Univ. Press, 1978, 301–328.

Enumerative checklist of works by and about Baraka.

Particularly strong in its treatment of primary materials, serving to update the thorough record of Item 30   as far as 1976.

BEECHER, JOHN (1904–1980)

37. Fraser, James. "John Beecher and his Rampart Press in Arizona: Homage to a Crusader." Arizona Librarian 24.1 (Winter 1967): 23–27.

Briefly descriptive account of the productions of Beecher's press from 1959 to 1963, including much of his own poetry.

BELITT, BEN (1911 –)

38. "Ben Belitt Bibliography and Checklist." Voyages 1.1 (Fall 1967): 31.

Brief account of selected works by Belitt.

BERRIGAN, DANIEL (1921 –)

39. Klejment, Anne. The Berrigans: A Bibliography of Published Works by Daniel, Philip, and Elizabeth McAlister Berrigan. New York: Garland, 1979.

Covers works by and about Berrigan through 1977. Primary sections provide informal descriptions of books, noting contents and first lines of poems. Index allows tracing of printing history of individual pieces. Secondary section is selective but annotated. Non-print materials excluded.

BERRY, WENDELL (1934 –)

40. Lalka, David G. Wendell Berry: A Descriptive Checklist. Macomb, Ill.: priv. pub., 1972.

Briefly descriptive treatment of printed works by Berry and
enumerative list of items about him.   Coverage through 1971.

41.   Hicks, Jack.   "A Wendell Berry Checklist."   Bulletin of Bibliography
37.3 (July-September 1980):   127-131.

Covers primary and secondary printed sources through early
1978.   Lists only uncollected poems, so that original printings
of collected pieces are not recorded.   Catalog of commentary on
Berry is unannotated.

BERRYMAN, JOHN   (1914-1972)

42.   Kelly, Richard J.   John Berryman: A Checklist.   Metuchen, N.J.:
Scarecrow Press, 1972.

Treats works by and about Berryman to 1972.   Coverage of
primary sources excludes non-print items and does not record
original periodical publication of poems later collected.
Secondary entries are not annotated.

43.   Stefanik, Ernest C., Jr.   John Berryman: A Preliminary Checklist.
Loyalhanna, Pa.:   priv. pub., 1972; 2nd ed.   Loyalhanna, Pa.:
priv. pub., 1972.

Thorough coverage of primary and secondary materials, with
notation of printing histories of individual poems.   Revised
versions of this work published as Items 44 and 45.

44.   _____.   "Bibliography: John Berryman Criticism."   West Coast
Review 8.2 (October 1973):   45-52.

Unannotated list of materials about Berryman through 1972,

organized by type of work (e.g., Biography, Homage, Book Reviews). Largely superseded by Item 49.

45. _____. "A John Berryman Checklist." <u>Bulletin of Bibliography</u> 31 (January-March 1974): 1-4, 28.

List of works by Berryman; superseded by Item 46.

46. _____. <u>John Berryman: A Descriptive Bibliography</u>. Pittsburgh: Univ. of Pittsburgh Press, 1974.

Exhaustive descriptive account of primary print and non-print materials. Provides detailed bibliographical history of individual poems, registering variants between book publications and noting reprintings in anthologies.

47. Kelly, Richard J., and Ernest C. Stefanik, Jr. "John Berryman: A Supplemental Checklist--Parts I-IV." <u>John Berryman Studies</u> 1.2 (April 1975): 25-35; 1.3 (July 1975): 23-31; 3.1 (Winter 1976): 48-50; 3.3 (Summer 1977): 36-48.

Designed to up-date the coverage of secondary materials provided by Item 42. Parts I-II were incorporated in Item 49; Parts III-IV superseded by Item 51.

48. Stefanik, Ernest C., Jr. "John Berryman: A Descriptive Bibliography--Addenda." <u>John Berryman Studies</u> 2.1 (Winter 1975): 38-47.

Supplements and up-dates Item 46.

49. Arpin, Gary Q. <u>John Berryman: A Reference Guide</u>. Boston: G. K. Hall, 1976.

Attempts complete coverage of secondary materials through 1974, except for non-critical sources noted in introduction. Arrangement is chronological; annotations summarize content of items.

50. Haffenden, John, and Richard J. Kelly. "John Berryman: Contributions to Periodicals & Annuals." John Berryman Studies 3.3 (Summer 1977): 49-51.

Supplements Item 46, listing pieces by Berryman not included there.

51. Kelly, Richard J. "John Berryman: A Ten Year Supplemental Checklist." Literary Research Newsletter 7.2-3 (Spring/Summer 1982): 65-115.

Supplements and up-dates into 1982 the enumerative record of primary and secondary materials provided by Item 42. Coverage is exhaustive but not annotated.

BISHOP, ELIZABETH (1911-1979)

52. MacMahon, Candace W. Elizabeth Bishop: A Bibliography 1927-1979. Charlottesville: Univ. Press of Virginia for the Bibliographical Society of the Univ. of Virginia, 1980.

Attempts an exhaustive record of both primary and secondary items. Sections covering different types of materials by Bishop are fully descriptive, with printing history of individual poems noted and variants carefully listed. Treatment of critical and biographical material about her is organized by category of commentary and is without significant annotation.

53.   Schwartz, Lloyd. "Bibliography, 1933-81." In Elizabeth Bishop and
         Her Art. Ed. Lloyd Schwartz and Sybil P. Estess. Ann Arbor:
         Univ. of Michigan Press, 1983, 331-341.
         Selective, enumerative checklist of primary and secondary
         publications, largely but not entirely displaced by Items 52
         and 54.

54.   Wyllie, Diana E. Elizabeth Bishop and Howard Nemerov: A Reference
         Guide. Boston: G. K. Hall, 1983.
         Selective account of primary works cannot compete with Item 52,
         but valuable for its chronological treatment of secondary ma-
         terials, with non-evaluative content notes for each item. Cov-
         erage through 1980.

BLACKBURN, PAUL   (1926-1971)

55.   Woodward, Kathleen. "Paul Blackburn Checklist." Schist 4/5 (1976-
         1978): 169-179.
         Preliminary account of Blackburn's books and anthology
         appearances. Superseded by Item 56.

56.   _____. Paul Blackburn: A Checklist. San Diego: Archive for
         New Poetry, Univ. of California, San Diego, 1980.
         A thorough account of primary materials, excluding only
         recordings and translations of Blackburn's work. Books are
         treated enumeratively, with brief notes about edition size.
         "Index to Poems" allows tracing of printing history of
         individual pieces.

BLASER, ROBIN (1925 -)

57. Nichols, Miriam, and Charles Watts. "A Robin Blaser Checklist."
     Line 3 (Spring 1984): 78-81.
     Enumerative treatment of works by Blaser into 1983, including
     broadsides and lost or destroyed titles.

BLY, ROBERT (1926 -)

58. McMillan, Samuel H. "On Robert Bly and His Poems: A Selected
     Bibliography." Tennessee Poetry Journal 2.2 (Winter 1969):
     58-60.
     Unannotated coverage of commentary on Bly through 1968.

59. Dorbin, Sandy. "Robert Bly Checklist." Schist 1 (Fall 1973): 48-
     51.
     Chronologically arranged list of primary works, including
     broadsides, into 1973. Limited coverage.

60. Friberg, Ingegerd. "Bibliography." In her Moving Inward: A Study
     of Robert Bly's Poetry. Gothenberg Studies in English, 38.
     Gothenberg, Sweden: Acta Universitatis Gothoburgensis, 1977,
     210-225.
     Records printed materials by and about Bly into 1975.
     Unorthodox arrangement separates similar types of publications
     into different sections. No annotations.

61. Doss, James, and Kate Daniels. "Selected Bibliography." In Of
     Solitude and Silence: Writings on Robert Bly. Ed. Richard
     Jones and Kate Daniels. Boston: Beacon Press, 1981, 268-276.
     A thorough but not exhaustive account of printed materials by

and about Bly into 1981. Treatment of primary works is enumerative but includes broadsides and posters. Secondary list furnishes fullest record available.

62. Roberson, William H. "Robert Bly: A Primary Bibliography, Part I."
     Bulletin of Bibliography 40.1 (March 1983): 5-11.
     Sound, enumerative catalog of Bly's separately issued works, including both fugitive print and non-print items, into 1983. Brief supplementary notes indicate size of editions and similar bibliographic information. See also Item 64.

63. Peseroff, Joyce. "Bibliography." In her Robert Bly: When Sleepers Awake. Ann Arbor: Univ. of Michigan Press, 1984, 335-345.
     Sound but selective checklist of materials by and about Bly into 1981. Primary coverage extends to his translations and tapes but excludes periodical appearances of poems. Secondary items include reviews.

64. Roberson, William H. "Robert Bly: A Primary Bibliography, Part II." Bulletin of Bibliography 41.2 (June 1984): 81-95.
     Complementing Item 62, furnishes a thorough list of Bly's periodical appearances, with separate, chronologically arranged sections for his poems and translations as well as for his numerous critical articles and essays. While some reprintings of items are noted, information on the subsequent appearance of pieces in collections and anthologies is not routinely provided.

BOWLES, PAUL (1911 -)

65. McLeod, Cecil R. <u>Paul Bowles: A Checklist 1929-1969</u>. N.p.: Apple
    Tree Press, 1970.

    Reliable treatment of primary printed materials, divided by
    type of work (e.g., Poetry, Translations, Music Reviews).
    Subsequent editions of books and reprintings of individual
    pieces noted.

BROOKS, GWENDOLYN (1917 -)

66. Loff, Jon N. "Gwendolyn Brooks: A Bibliography." <u>CLA Journal</u>
    17.1 (September 1973): 21-32.

    Account of primary (including non-print) and secondary
    materials through 1972. The unannotated list of commentary on
    Brooks largely superseded by Item 68.

67. Mahoney, Heidi L. "Selected Checklist of Material By and About
    Gwendolyn Brooks." <u>Negro American Literature Forum</u> 8.2
    (Summer 1974): 210-211.

    Limited coverage to 1972, distinguished only by brief notation
    of some manuscript holdings.

68. Miller, R. Baxter. <u>Langston Hughes and Gwendolyn Brooks: A Refer-</u>
    <u>ence Guide</u>. Boston: G. K. Hall, 1978.

    Provides annotated coverage of writings about Brooks through
    1977. Notes restate content and point-of-view of items.
    Volume has been severely criticized for omissions and errors:
    see, e.g., <u>Resources for American Literary Study</u> 10.1 (Spring
    1980): 84-88.

BUKOWSKI, CHARLES (1920 -)

69. Dorbin, Sanford. A Bibliography of Charles Bukowski. Los Angeles: Black Sparrow Press, 1969.

Comprehensively covers works by and about Bukowski into 1969. Fully describes separate publications, even ephemerae, with supplementary notes furnishing further bibliographical information, including notation of different printings of individual poems. Secondary section lightly annotated. See also Dorbin's "Bukowski Bibliography Revisited" in Small Press Review 16 (May 1973): 23-31.

70. Fox, Hugh. Charles Bukowski: A Critical and Bibliographical Study. Somerville, Mass.: Abyss Publications, 1969, esp. 96-121. Restricted to periodical appearances of Bukowski's work. Not as thorough as Item 69 but occasionally notes items missed there.

CHAMBERS, GEORGE (1931 -)

71. "Bibliography." Voyages to the Inland Sea 4 (1974): 52-54. Chronological list of works by Chambers into 1973. Predominantly magazine appearances.

CHAPPELL, FRED (1936 -)

72. Kibler, James Everett, Jr. "A Fred Chappell Bibliography, 1963-1983." Mississippi Quarterly 37.1 (Winter 1983-1984): 63-88. Provides very thorough coverage of Chappell's printed works as well as a record of writings about him. Excluding only the juvenalia, the enumerative coverage of primary materials cites both original and subsequent appearances of individual items,

so that their publication histories can be easily determined. The occurrence of revisions between different printings is also noted.

CHATFIELD, HALE (1936 -)

73. "Hale Chatfield--Bibliography." Voyages to the Inland Sea 7 (1977): 27-32.

Sound coverage of primary sources into 1977.

CIARDI, JOHN (1916 -)

74. White, William. John Ciardi: A Bibliography. Detroit: Wayne State Univ. Press, 1959.

Covers printed works by and about Ciardi into 1959. Treatment of books is fully descriptive. Relation between periodical and book publication of poems not remarked but traceable through the index. Secondary items not annotated.

CLARK, TOM (1941 -)

75. Murray, Timothy. "Tom Clark: A Checklist." Credences: A Journal of Twentieth Century Poetry and Poetics N.S. 1.1 (1981): 121-165.

Exacting, enumerative treatment of works by Clark as well as a list of articles about him. Notes provide printing information and indicate contents. Coverage extends into early 1980.

CONGDON, KIRBY (1924 -)

76. Kirby Congdon: A Bibliography of Separate Publications 1947-1980. New York: Interim Books, 1980.

Briefly descriptive treatment of separately published works by
Congdon, including broadsides and ephemerae, through 1980.

COOLEY, PETER (1940 -)

77. "Peter Cooley: Publications." Voyages to the Inland Sea 5 (1975):
25-27.

Checklist of primary materials into 1975.

COOLIDGE, CLARK (1939 -)

78. "Biblio: Coolidge." Stations 5 (Winter 1978): 30.

Brief checklist of works by Coolidge through 1976, including
anthology publications, broadsides, and recordings.

CORMAN, CID (1924 -)

79. Lepper, Gary M. "A Cid Corman Checklist." Issued as a supplement
to Madrona 11-12 (December 1975).

Briefly descriptive checklist of separately published books by
Corman, including translations.

CORSO, GREGORY (1930 -)

80. Wilson, Robert A. A Bibliography of Works by Gregory Corso: 1954-
1965. New York: Phoenix Book Shop, 1966.

An informally descriptive account of primary materials,
including drawings and recordings, through 1965. Neither
contents of collected volumes nor subsequent printings of items
published in magazines noted.

COXE, LOUIS (1918 -)

81. Coxe, Louis. "A Checklist of the Writings of Louis Coxe."
Princeton University Library Chronicle 25.1 (Autumn 1963):

16-20.

Sound coverage of published work by Coxe through mid-1963.

CREELEY, ROBERT   (1926 -)

82.   Rodefer, Stephen.   "A Workable Bibliography of Robert Creeley."
      whe're 1 (Summer 1966):   58-60.

      List of poems published by Creeley between 1962 and 1966, in
      the order of their presumed composition.

83.   Johnson, Lee Ann.   "Robert Creeley: A Checklist 1946-1970."
      Twentieth Century Literature 17.3 (1971):   181-198.

      Treats works by and about Creeley through 1970.   Primary
      section is enumerative, with informal descriptive notes;
      includes non-print items but excludes most anthology
      appearances.   Secondary section is not annotated.

84.   Calhoun, Douglas.   "Robert Creeley: A Critical Checklist Part II:
      A Checklist."   West Coast Review 6.3 (January 1972):   64-71.

      Thorough, but unannotated coverage of commentary on Creeley
      into 1971.   Includes numerous "trivial" references not in
      either Item 85 or 86.   Organized alphabetically by critic.

85.   Novik, Mary.   "Robert Creeley: A Critical Checklist Part I:
      Criticism, 1950-1970."   West Coast Review 6.3 (January 1972):
      51-63.

      A selective account of commentary on Creeley into early 1971,
      awkwardly arranged by type of publication, so that essays in
      books and those in periodicals are entered in different

sections. General comments and superficial reviews excluded; no annotations.

86. _____. Robert Creeley: An Inventory, 1945-1970. Kent, Ohio: Kent State Univ. Press; Montreal: McGill-Queen's Univ. Press, 1973.

Provides exhaustive coverage of primary materials (including non-print items and manuscripts) and selective treatment of secondary sources through 1970. Enumerative presentation of separately issued works supplemented with detailed notes covering physical description and publishing history. Very thorough tracing of publication history of individual poems and prose pieces, with references to manuscripts. Secondary section retains the organization of Item 85 but the number of references included is greatly expanded.

87. Murray, Timothy, and Stephen Boardway. "Year by Year Bibliography of Robert Creeley." In Robert Creeley: The Poet's Workshop. Ed. Carroll F. Terrell. Orono, Me.: National Poetry Foundation, 1984, 313-374.

Enumerative treatment of Creeley's printed works of prose and poetry, including periodical appearances and broadsides, is presented chronologically, with coverage extending from 1940 through 1983. Supplements Item 86.

CUNNINGHAM, J. V. (1911 -)

88. Gullans, Charles. A Bibliography of the Published Works of J. V. Cunningham. Los Angeles: Univ. of California Library, Los Angeles, 1973.

Fully descriptive account of primary publications, excluding anthology and textbook reprints. Notes and indexes allow tracing of publication history of individual works. Appendix furnishes composition dates of poems. Coverage is through 1971.

DANA, ROBERT (1929 -)

89. "Bibliography." Voyages to the Inland Sea 3 (1973): 81-83.

Records works by and reviews of Dana into 1973. Primary coverage includes periodical publications but does not note subsequent printings.

DICKEY, JAMES (1923 -)

90. Glancy, Eileen K. "James Dickey: A Bibliography." Twentieth Century Literature 15.1 (April 1969): 45-61.

Registers primary and secondary printed materials into 1969. Sections on periodical appearances of individual pieces note subsequent book publication. Incorporated in Item 91.

91. _____. James Dickey: The Critic as Poet, An Annotated Bibliography With an Introductory Essay. Troy, N.Y.: Whitson Publishing Co., 1971.

Enumerative treatment of works by and about Dickey into 1970. Primary coverage omits non-print materials, broadsides, and published emphemerae. Short annotations in secondary section indicate arguments of items.

92. Ashley, Franklin. James Dickey: A Checklist. Detroit: Gale Research Co., 1972.

Coverage of primary sources into 1972. Brief physical descriptions of books, accompanied by reproductions of title pages. Marred by variety of minor errors, noted in preface of Item 94.

93. Hill, Robert W. "James Dickey: A Checklist." In James Dickey: The Expansive Imagination, A Collection of Critical Essays. Ed. Richard J. Calhoun. Deland, Fla.: Everett/Edwards, 1973, 213-228.

Specifically designed to supplement, correct, and up-date Item 90. Provides coverage of items by and about Dickey into 1972.

94. Elledge, Jim. James Dickey: A Bibliography, 1947-1974. Metuchen, N.J.: Scarecrow Press, 1979.

Accounts for materials by and about Dickey through 1974. Primary section includes non-print items but not broadsides or emphemerae; treatment is enumerative, with no printing history. Secondary section awkwardly arranged by type of publication but is thorough, with informative annotations. Organization throughout is idiosyncratic but good indexes compensate.

95. Fritz, Donald E., and Patricia De La Fuente. "James Dickey: An Updated Checklist of Scholarship, 1975-1978." In James Dickey: Splintered Sunlight: Interviews, Essays, and Bibliography. Ed. Patricia De La Fuente, Donald E. Fritz, and Jan Seale. Edinburg, Tex.: School of Humanities, Pan American University, 1979, 65-74.

Supplements Item 94 with unannotated coverage of secondary

items (including interviews) from 1975 through 1978. Largely
superseded by Item 96.

96. Elledge, Jim. "James Dickey: A Supplementary Bibliography, 1975-
1980." Bulletin of Bibliography 38.2 (April-June 1981):   92-
100, 104, 38.3 (July-September 1981):   150-155.
Updates primary and secondary coverage of Item 94 through 1980.

97. Wright, Stuart. James Dickey: A Bibliography of His Books,
Pamphlets, and Broadsides. Dallas, Tex.: Pressworks, 1982.
Exhaustive physical descriptions of the first editions of
Dickey's separately printed works through 1981. Later editions
briefly noted. No account of periodical appearances or non-
print materials. Within its limits, replaces Item 92.

DODSON, OWEN (1914 -)

98. Hatch, James V., Douglas A. M. Ward, and Joe Weixlmann. "The Rungs
of a Powerful Long Ladder: An Owen Dodson Bibliography."
Black American Literature Forum 14.2 (Summer 1980): 60-68.
Thorough record of materials by (including non-print items) and
about Dodson into early 1980. Treatment of primary sources
includes broadsides and ephemerae but catalog of periodical
publications does not indicate subsequent printings. Secondary
coverage is unannotated.

DORN, EDWARD (1929 -)

99. Butterick, George F. "Edward Dorn: A Checklist." Athanor 5
(Winter 1973): 51-68.
Reliable account of works both by and about Dorn into 1972,

including non-print and ephemeral materials.

100. Streeter, David. A Bibliography of Ed Dorn. New York: Phoenix
      Bookshop, 1973 (c. 1974).

      Provides detailed treatment of primary materials through 1972.
      Basic physical description of books; index allows tracing of
      printing history of individual poems.

DUNCAN, ROBERT (1919 -)

101. Bertholf, Robert J. Robert Duncan: A Descriptive Bibliography.
      Santa Barbara, Calif.: Black Sparrow Press, [forthcoming
      1986].

      Provides exhaustive descriptions of Duncan's primary works,
      including periodical appearances and ephemerae. Equally
      thorough but unannotated accounting of secondary materials.

ECKMAN, FREDERICK (1924 -)

102. Angst, Bim, Gerald Burnsteel, and Frederick Eckman. "Frederick
      Eckman: A Selected Checklist." In The Continental Connection:
      Selected Writings of Frederick Eckman, 1947-1980. Ed. Gerald
      Burnsteel and Bim Angst. Ann Arbor: Itinerary, 1980, 185-189.
      Enumerative record of Eckman's books, editorial work, and
      uncollected prose; numerous contributions of poems to little
      magazines not recorded.

EIGNER, LARRY (1927 -)

103. Wyatt, Andrea. A Bibliography of Works by Larry Eigner 1937-1969.
      Berkeley: Oyez, 1970.

      Covers printed works by Eigner through 1969. Books are briefly described, with content notes recording both titles and first lines of poems. Index allows tracing of publishing history of individual works.

ELLIOTT, HARLEY (1940 -)

104. "Bibliography of Publications: Harley Elliott." _Voyages to the Inland Sea_ 6 (1976): 27-34.

Full record of primary printed sources into 1976.

ETTER, DAVE (1928 -)

105. "Bibliography." _Voyages to the Inland Sea_ 1 (1971): 71-72.

Selected list of works by and about Etter into 1970. No record of magazine publications. Secondary coverage most useful.

EVERSON, WILLIAM (1912 -)

106. Kherdian, David. "Brother Antoninus." In his _Six Poets of the San Francisco Renaissance: Portraits and Checklists_. Fresno, Calif.: Giligia Press, 1967, 131-183, esp. 153-183.

Provides sound coverage of works by and about Everson through 1966. Primary sections are enumerative, with informal notes furnishing physical descriptions and bibliographical history. Secondary section is briefly annotated.

107. Bartlett, Lee, and Allan Campo. _William Everson: A Descriptive Bibliography 1934-1976_. Metuchen, N.J.: Scarecrow Press, 1977.

Records both primary (printed only) and secondary materials through 1976. Furnishes basic description of works by Everson, including ephemeral items; supplementary notes give further bibliographical information. Secondary section is selective and not annotated.

FERLINGHETTI, LAWRENCE (1919 -)

108. Kherdian, David. "Lawrence Ferlinghetti." In his Six Poets of the San Francisco Renaissance: Portraits and Checklists. Fresno, Calif.: Giligia Press, 1967, 3-44, esp. 9-44.

Sound coverage of works by and about Ferlinghetti into 1966. Enumerative treatment supplemented by informal descriptive notes and brief annotations.

109. Morgan, Bill. Lawrence Ferlinghetti: A Comprehensive Bibliography to 1980. New York: Garland, 1982.

Exhaustive account of works by and about Ferlinghetti through 1980. Primary coverage extends to non-print and ephemeral materials, excluding only editorial and publicity work. Physical descriptions of books, pamphlets, and broadsides highly detailed, with supplementary notes providing histories. The printing histories of individual poems also furnished, including notation of the extent of revision between different appearances. Secondary section is equally comprehensive but without annotations.

GALLER, DAVID (1929 -)

110. "Checklist of Work by David Galler." Voyages 3.3-4 (Spring 1970): 93.

Abbreviated coverage of primary sources (including non-print), principally of value for its record of magazines containing poems by Galler.

GARRETT, GEORGE (1929 -)

111. Garrett, George, Thomas L. McHaney, and James B. Meriwether. "A
      Checklist of the Writings of George Garrett." Princeton
      University Library Chronicle 25.1 (Autumn 1963): 33-39.
      Thorough, enumerative treatment of work by Garrett, including
      unpublished scripts, into late 1963.

112. George Palmer Garrett: A Bibliography and Index of His Published
      Works and Criticism of Them. Potsdam: Frederick W. Crumb
      Mcmorial Library, State Univ. College, 1968.
      Primary and secondary checklist into 1968. Unannotated and
      based on citations from standard indexes only.

113. Dillard, R. H. W. "George Garrett: A Checklist of His Writings."
      Mill Mountain Review (Summer 1971): 221-234.
      Enumerative coverage of primary sources into 1971, including
      record of separate publication of poems and essays, though
      subsequent appearances in collections and anthologies not
      noted. Unpublished screenplays listed.

114. Wright, Stuart. "George Garrett: A Bibliographic Chronicle, 1947-
      1980." Bulletin of Bibliography 38.1 (January-March 1981):
      6-19, 25.
      Thorough accounting of both primary and secondary printed
      sources through 1980. Section treating works by Garrett is a
      chronological record, with collected and republished
      appearances of individual items regularly noted. Unannotated
      treatment of commentary on Garrett.

GINSBERG, ALLEN (1926 -)

115. Menkin, Edward Z. "Allen Ginsberg: A Bibliography and Biographical
        Sketch." Thoth 8.3 (Winter 1967): 35-44, esp. 41-44.
        Selective checklist of primary and secondary items into 1965.

116. Dowden, George. A Bibliography of Works by Allen Ginsberg, October,
        1943 to July 1, 1967. San Franicsco: City Lights Books, 1971.
        Treats the full range of primary materials, including many
        types of non-print sources. Both the arrangement of sections
        and the style of physical description are idiosyncratic.
        Despite unorthodox methods, provides a wealth of information
        about the publishing circumstances and history of Ginsberg's
        work, which is rendered more accessible by Laurence McGilvery's
        indexes. Contrary to the title, coverage extends to 1968.

117. Kraus, Michelle P. Allen Ginsberg: An Annotated Bibliography,
        1969-1977. Metuchen, N.J.: Scarecrow Press, 1980.
        Supplementing Item 116, brings the record to early 1978 but
        covers both primary and secondary works. Treatment of primary
        materials is essentially enumerative, its lack of detail
        severely limiting utility, especially for tracing the history
        of printed items. Notes throughout focus on content, which
        renders the sections on secondary sources particularly
        valuable.

118. Selerie, Gavin. "Allen Ginsberg--A Selective Bibliography." In his
        Allen Ginsberg. Riverside Interviews, 1. London: Binnacle
        Press, 1980, 43-51.

Limited checklist of both primary and secondary materials that usefully carries coverage into 1980. Supplements Item 117.

GOODMAN, PAUL (1911-1972)

119. Glassheim, Eliot. "Paul Goodman: A Checklist, 1931-1971." Bulletin of Bibliography and Magazine Notes 29.2 (April-June 1972): 61-72.

Enumerative record of printed materials by and about Goodman. Fully superseded by Item 121.

120. Nicely, Tom. "Notes Toward a Bibliography: The Chief References and Checklist of the Published Stories." New Letters 42.2-3 (Winter-Spring 1976): 246-253.

Bibliographic essay treats selected secondary sources; coverage of stories deliberately revises and updates treatment provided by Item 119; reprints are regularly noted.

121. _____. Adam and His Work: A Bibliography of Sources By and About Paul Goodman (1911-1972). Metuchen, N.J.: Scarecrow Press, 1979.

Exhaustive account of primary and secondary sources, including non-print, ephemeral, and other specialized sources, through 1978. Major section covering works by Goodman is arranged chronologically and provides brief physical description with full printing history of separately published works. Thorough listing of commentary on Goodman, extending to brief "mentions," is only occasionally annotated.

GREENBERG, ALVIN (1932 -)

122. "Bibliography of Poems Published." Voyages to the Inland Sea 4
    (1974): 31-34.

    Primary checklist, including magazine publications, into 1973.

HARRISON, JIM (1937 -)

123. Colonnese, Tom. "Jim Harrison: A Checklist." Bulletin of
    Bibliography 39.3 (September 1982): 132-135.

    Enumerative treatment through 1981 of primary and secondary
    printed sources. Coverage restricted to citations from
    standard indexes and bibliographic data bases and consequently
    excludes important little magazine material.

HAYDEN, ROBERT (1913-1980)

124. Nicholas, Xavier. "Robert Hayden: A Bibliography." Obsidian 7.1
    (Spring 1981): 109-127.

    Provides thorough, enumerative treatment of published materials
    both by and about Hayden. Primary section indicates subsequent
    revision and republication of individual poems. Secondary
    section is unannotated but scrupulously inclusive.

125. _____. "Robert Hayden: A Bibliography." Obsidian 8.1
    (Spring 1982): 207-210.

    Supplements Item 124, adding overlooked items and bringing
    coverage forward into 1981.

HEARST, JAMES (1910 -)

126. "Bibliography of James Schell Hearst." Voyages to the Inland Sea 2
    (1972): 52-61.

Coverage of primary materials, including recordings, into 1972.
Notes original and subsequent printings of individual poems.

HEYEN, WILLIAM (1940 -)

127. Stefanik, Ernest. "William Heyen: A Descriptive Checklist."
Bulletin of Bibliography 36.4 (October-December 1979): 157-176.

Attempts a complete listing of works by and about Heyen through
mid-1979. Enumerative handling of separate works, including
broadsides and ephemerae, is supplemented by notes describing
publishing circumstances. Though reprintings of poems first
appearing in periodicals are recorded, their inclusions in
Heyen's own collections not noted. Secondary section is
unannotated.

HIGGINS, DICK (1938 -)

128. "Selective Bibliography of Dick Higgins' Work." Spanner 9 (January
1977): 185-192.

Enumerative checklist of primary sources through 1975,
including anthology appearances, periodical contributions, and
ephemeral publications. Brief list of critical articles on
Higgins as well as data on his exhibitions also provided.

HOFFMAN, DANIEL (1923 -)

129. "A Daniel Hoffman Checklist." Voyages 3.1-2 (Winter 1970): 119.
Briefly lists principal works by Hoffman.

130. Lowe, Michael. Daniel Hoffman: A Comprehensive Bibliography. Norwood, Pa.: Norwood Editions, 1973.

Treats both primary and secondary sources into 1973. Sections
on different types of works by Hoffman are enumerative but
thorough in coverage, with reprinting of pieces noted. Section
listing commentary about Hoffman is similarly exacting but
without annotations. Absence of index reduces usefulness of
the volume.

HOLMES, JOHN CLELLON (1926 -)

131. Ardinger, Richard K. An Annotated Bibliography of Works by John
      Clellon Holmes. Pocatello: Idaho State Univ. Press, 1979.
      Descriptive account of primary sources through 1978. Numerous
      entries accompanied by comments by Holmes on the circumstances
      of composition and publication.

HOLMES, THEODORE (1928 -)

132. Brogan, James. "A Checklist of the Writings of Theodore Holmes."
      Princeton University Library Chronicle 25.1 (Autumn 1963):
      50-51.
      Coverage of primary texts through 1961.

HUGO, RICHARD (1923-1982)

133. Ives, George. Bibliography in "Richard Hugo Issue." Slackwater
      Review (1978): 179-187.
      Enumerative list of primary and secondary materials, with
      annotations of longer critical pieces by and about Hugo.
      Superseded by Items 134 and 135.

134. Allen, Michael. "Richard Hugo: A Bibliography." In A Trout in the
      Milk: A Composite Portrait of Richard Hugo. Ed. Jack Myers.

Lewiston, Idaho: Confluence Press, 1982, 315-334.

Reliably lists primary and secondary publications into 1977, though some items as late as 1980 are entered.   Both primary and secondary coverage organized by type of publication; subsequent appearance of individual poems not noted.

135.   Bense, James.   "Richard Hugo: A Bibliography."   Bulletin of Bibliography 40.3 (September 1983):   148-162.

A thorough enumerative record of writings by and about Hugo, compiled independently of Item 134.   Chronologically arranged primary section extends into 1982, specifying subsequent publication of single items in collections and anthologies.   Unannotated secondary section includes items as late as 1983. Updates but does not fully replace Item 134, which still contains unique items.

IGNATOW, DAVID (1914 -)

136.   Smith, Roberta K.   David Ignatow, Poet: A Checklist of Writings (Partial).   Storrs: Univ. of Connecticut Library, 1966.

Provides enumerative coverage into 1966 of primary publications, including books, poems in periodicals, and reviews.   Unannotated and incomplete.

137.   Lipari, Joseph Anthony.   "The Poetry of David Ignatow: An Introduction and Bibliography of Primary Sources, 1931-1978." Diss. Washington State University 1983.

Exhaustive treatment of works by Ignatow through 1978.   Books are fully described; contributions to periodicals and books are listed as are broadsides.

IRBY, KENNETH   (1936 -   )

138.   Bertholf, Robert. "Kenneth Irby: A Checklist." Credences 3.1
         (February 1979): 142-149.
         Covers works by and about Irby through 1978. Enumerative
         treatment of primary sources, with supplemental notes for
         printing facts.

JARRELL, RANDALL   (1914-1965)

139.   Adams, Charles M. Randall Jarrell: A Bibliography. Chapel Hill:
         Univ. of North Carolina Press, 1958.
         A thorough record of primary printed texts through 1957. Full
         descriptions of separately published books. Alphabetically
         organized sections on individual poems and prose pieces provide
         chronological accounts of each item's published appearances,
         though variants are not noted.

140.   _____. "A Supplement to Randall Jarrell: A Bibliography."
         Analects 1.2 (Spring 1961): 49-56.
         Continues the coverage of primary materials in Item 139 for the
         period 1958 through 1960, with identical level of descriptive
         detail.

141.   Kisslinger, Margaret V. "A Bibliography of Randall Jarrell."
         Bulletin of Bibliography and Magazine Notes 24.10 (May-August
         1966): 243-247.
         Intended to supplement Item 139, provides enumerative coverage
         of primary and secondary sources printed during the period
         1958-1965. Unconventionally arranged, with critical commentary
         specific to individual poems or books of poetry integrated with

entry for Jarrell's text. No connections drawn between periodical appearances of poems and their inclusion in collections. Selected secondary pieces are annotated.

142. Adams, Charles M. "A Bibliographical Excursion with Some Biographical Footnotes on Randall Jarrell." Bulletin of Bibliography and Magazine Notes 28.3 (July-September 1971): 79-81.

Treats juvenalia excluded from Item 139.

143. Gillikin, Dure Jo. "A Checklist of Criticism on Randall Jarrell 1941-1970, With an Introduction and a List of His Major Works." New York Public Library Bulletin 75.4 (April 1971): 176-194. Brief list of separately published works by Jarrell and an unannotated record of discussions about him, through 1970. Supersedes secondary aspects of Item 141.

144. Meyers, Jeffrey. "Randall Jarrell: A Bibliography of Criticism, 1941-1981." Bulletin of Bibliography 39.4 (December 1982): 227-234.

Restricted to "substantial reviews and significant references," thus excluding numerous shorter pieces listed in Item 143, but recording French and German materials neglected there. Arrangement is alphabetical by critic, with all citations-- including reviews--in a single sequence. Though reviews are identified generically, absence of annotations makes it impossible to connect particular reviews to their specific books.

145. Wilson, Robert A. "Randall Jarrell: A Bibliographical Checklist."
      American Book Collector 3.3 (May–June 1982): 32–40.
      Treats only first editions of separately published works by, or
      with contributions from, Jarrell through 1980. Brief physical
      description for each item. Partially up-dates Items 139 and
      140.

146. Wright, Stuart T. Randall Jarrell: A Descriptive Bibliography,
      1929–1983. Charlottesville: Univ. of Virginia Press for the
      Bibliographical Society of the Univ. of Virginia, [forthcoming
      1985, c. 1984].
      Promises to supersede all previous accounts of Jarrell's
      published work.

KELLY, ROBERT (1935 –)

147. Rasula, Jed. "Robert Kelly: A Checklist." Credences NS 3.1
      (Spring 1984): 91–124.
      Exhaustive coverage of printed works by Kelly into 1983.
      Treatment of separate publications is enumerative but
      supplementary notes describe publishing circumstances and
      supply related bibliographical information. Subsequent
      collection of individually published poems not, however,
      specified.

KEROUAC, JACK (1922–1969)

148. Charters, Ann. A Bibliography of Works by Jack Kerouac (Jean Louis
      Lebris De Kerouac) 1939–1967. New York: Phoenix Book Shop
      1967. Rev. ed. New York: Phoenix Bookshop, 1975.
      Descriptive coverage of primary sources, including non-print

materials.   Index allows tracing of publication history of individual poems.   Revised edition corrects original work and brings record through 1975.

149. Bierkins, Jef. "Supplement to William Gargan's `Jack Kerouac: Biography and Criticism--A Working Bibliography': Works in the Dutch Language." <u>Moody Street Irregulars</u> 8 (Summer/Fall 1980): 18.

Supplements Item 150, recording Dutch responses to Kerouac published from 1963 through 1979.

150. Gargan, William. "Jack Kerouac: Biography and Criticism--A Working Bibliography." <u>Moody Street Irregulars</u> 6/7 (Winter/Spring 1980): 21-23.

Provides unannotated listing of secondary materials into 1979, including little magazine and foreign language items.

151. Nisonger, Thomas Evans. "Jack Kerouac: A Bibliography of Biographical and Critical Material, 1950-1979." <u>Bulletin of Bibliography</u> 37.1 (January-March 1980): 23-32.

Unannotated coverage of secondary sources through 1979. Arranged by type of commentary, with separate sections for articles, books, reviews, etc. Scope not as extensive as Item 152 but lists numerous items lacking there.

152. Milewski, Robert J. <u>Jack Kerouac: An Annotated Bibliography of Secondary Sources, 1944-1979</u>. Metuchen, N.J.: Scarecrow Press, 1981.

Broad but uneven treatment of secondary references through

1979. Organization by genre of criticism is supplemented by index. Notes accompanying most entries summarize theme or argument of the piece.

153. Poteet, Maurice. "A Select Québec-France Bibliography sur Kerouac." Moody Street Irregulars 11 (Spring/Summer 1982): 7-9. Lists and briefly annotates, in English, French-language commentary on Kerouac from 1963-1980.

KINNELL, GALWAY (1927 -)

154. Hawkins, Sherman. "A Checklist of the Writings of Galway Kinnell." Princeton University Library Chronicle 25.1 (Autumn 1963): 65-70. Thorough, enumerative list of primary sources into 1963.

155. Galway Kinnell: A Bibliography and Index of His Published Works and Criticism of Them. Potsdam, N.Y.: Frederick W. Crumb Memorial Library, State Univ. College, 1968. Records works by and about Kinnell into 1967, including periodical appearances of individual poems.

156. Stutz, Linda. "Bibliography for Galway Kinnell." Stone Drum 1.2 (Fall 1972): 34-39. Extensive coverage of primary and secondary printed sources through 1971. Treats original magazine publications but does not note later printings.

157. Ewert, William B., and Barbara A. White. "Galway Kinnell: A Bibliographical Checklist." American Book Collector NS 5.4

(July–August 1984):   22–32; NS 6.1 (January–February 1985):
31–35.

Fully descriptive analysis of the first and bibliographically
significant later editions of separately published works by
Kinnell into 1984, including translations and anthology
appearances. Periodical publications excluded.

KLOEFKORN, WILLIAM

158. "William Kloefkorn--Bibliography." Voyages to the Inland Sea 7
(1977):   58–62.

Primary coverage through 1976.

KNOEPFLE, JOHN   (1923 -)

159. "Bibliography." Voyages to the Inland Sea 1 (1971):   45.

Secondary checklist into 1970.

KOOSER, TED   (1939 -)

160. "Ted Kooser." Voyages to the Inland Sea 6 (1976):   60–69.

Thorough coverage of works by and about Kooser into 1976.

KUMIN, MAXINE   (1925 -)

161. Bickers, Arleen Phillips. "A Bibliography of the Works of Maxine W.
Kumin: 1960–1980." M. A. Thesis Memphis State Univ. 1982.
Exhaustive treatment of primary published sources is
accompanied by annotated list of secondary materials. Books
are described and periodical publication of individual poems
and prose writings fully traced.

LAX, ROBERT   (1915 -)

162. "A Checklist of Books by Robert Lax Published by Emil Antonucci."

<u>Voyages</u> 2.1-2 (Winter-Spring 1968):   99.

Also includes films done by Lax working with Antonucci.   In addition, "A Short Biographical Sketch of Robert Lax" on p. 6 of this issue has bibliographical interest.

<u>LEVERTOV, DENISE</u>   (1923 -   )

163. Wilson, Robert. <u>A Bibliography of Denise Levertov</u>.   New York: Phoenix Book Shop, 1972.

A thorough account of primary materials, including recordings and ephemerae, into late 1972.   Treatment of separately published works is fully descriptive.   Index allows tracing of printing history of single works.

<u>LEVINE, PHILIP</u>   (1928 -   )

164. Cobb, Jeffrey B. "Philip Levine: A Bibliographical Checklist." <u>American Book Collector</u> NS 6.2 (March-April 1985): 38-47. Provides full descriptive treatment of separately published primary texts into 1984, including pamphlets, broadsides, and appearances in anthologies.   Periodical publications excluded.

<u>LIFSHIN, LYN</u>   (1942 -   )

165. Malone, Marvin. "The Beginning of an Annotated Bibliography for Lyn Lifshin." <u>Wormwood Review</u> 15.3 (1975): 97-104. Enumerates and furnishes informal descriptions of Lifshin's books into 1975 as well as various "special items" (e.g., first periodical appearance, special magazine issues, first broadside).   Useful, despite limited scope.

LOGAN, JOHN (1923 -)

166. "John Logan Bibliography." <u>Voyages</u> 4.3-4 (Spring 1971-Spring
      1972): 51-53.
      Brief lists of the principal works by and about Logan to 1971.
      Does not record periodical appearances of poems and excludes
      non-print materials.

LOWELL, ROBERT (1917-1977)

167. Staples, Hugh. "Robert Lowell: Bibliography 1939-1959, with an
      Illustrative Critique." <u>Harvard Library Bulletin</u> 13 (Spring
      1959): 292-318.
      Furnishes an account of printed sources by and about Lowell
      into 1959. Enumerative treatment of primary works focuses on
      variant published versions of individual poems. Secondary
      sections exclude foreign material and are not annotated.

168. Mazzaro, Jerome. <u>The Achievement of Robert Lowell: 1939-1959</u>.
      Detroit: Univ. of Detroit Press, 1960.
      Thorough record of printed materials by and about Lowell
      through 1959 (including some non-English items). Descriptive
      handling of separately published works. Variants among
      different appearances of single poems exactly noted.
      Unannotated secondary section divided topically. This is an
      expanded and revised version of an article of identical title
      issued in <u>Fresco</u> 10 (Winter-Spring 1960): 51-77. Largely
      supersedes Item 167.

169. Staples, Hugh. "Appendix II: Bibliography." In his <u>Robert Lowell:
      The First Twenty Years</u>. New York: Farrar, Straus and Cudahy;

London: Faber and Faber, 1962, 108-115.

Revised version of Item 167, with secondary coverage dropped
and greater attention to primary works, which are presented
enumeratively into 1961.

170.   Mazzaro, Jerome. "Checklist: 1939-1968." In Robert Lowell: A
Portrait of the Artist in His Time. Ed. Michael London and
Robert Boyers. New York: David Lewis, 1970, 293-328.
Unannotated but extensive listing of secondary materials,
divided categorically (e.g., Interviews, Biography, Criticism).
For discussions of Lowell, supersedes Item 168.

171.   Zin, Annamaria. "Italian Bibliography on Robert Lowell." In Robert
Lowell: A Tribute. Ed. Roland Anzilotti. Pisa: Nistri-
Lischi Editori, 1979, 172-180.
Treatment of Italian translations of Lowell's work and of
Italian commentary on it through 1977.

172.   Axelrod, Steven Gould, and Helen Deese. Robert Lowell: A Reference
Guide. Boston: G. K. Hall, 1982.
Exhaustive, chronologically organized coverage of secondary
materials in English through 1980, excluding only creative
works and insignificant commentary in textbooks and
anthologies. Annotations effectively restate argument or
summarize content of each item.

MAC LOW, JACKSON (1922 -)

173.   "Mac Low Bibliography." Paper Air 2.3 (1980):   63-65.

Enumerative list of primary materials, including scores and non-print items, through 1980.

MAJOR, CLARENCE (1936 -)

174. Weixlmann, Joe. "Clarence Major: A Checklist of Criticism." _Obsidian_ 4.2 (1978): 101-113.

Thorough coverage of secondary writings through 1976. According to Item 175, marred by "numerous publisher's errors."

175. _____, and Clarence Major. "Toward a Primary Bibliography of Clarence Major." _Black American Literature Forum_ 13.2 (Summer 1979): 70-72.

Record of printed works by Major into 1979. Periodical appearances of individual poems not cataloged.

MARIAH, PAUL (1937 -)

176. Rice, Raymond. "The Child Is Father to the Man: A Preliminary Bibliography of the Poetry of Paul Mariah (1965-1970)." _Margins_ 20 (May 1975): 36-39.

Briefly annotated checklist of primary printed materials published in the period 1965-1970.

MATHEWS, HARRY (1930 -)

177. "Harry Mathews: A Bibliography." _Juillard_ (Winter 1968-1969): n. pag.

Enumerative treatment of primary works through 1968, including Mathews' work as a translator.

MCCLURE, MICHAEL (1932 -)

78. Clements, Marshall. _A Catalog of Works by Michael McClure 1956-

1965. New York: Phoenix Book Shop, 1965.

Brief descriptive treatment of primary works. Largely

superseded by Item 179.

179. Kherdian, David. "Michael McClure." In his <u>Six Poets of the San
Francisco Renaissance: Portraits and Checklists</u>. Fresno,
Calif.: Giligia Press, 1967, 109-129, esp. 115-129.

Covers thoroughly both primary materials (including ephemeral
and non-print items) and secondary commentary into 1966.
Enumerative treatment supplemented by informal descriptive and
content notes.

<u>MCGRATH, THOMAS</u> (1916 -)

180. "Selected Bibliography." <u>Voyages to the Inland Sea</u> 3 (1973): 63-
64.

Checklist of books, anthology appearances, and tapes of McGrath
into 1973. Periodical publications excluded.

<u>MELTZER, DAVID</u> (1937 -)

181. Kherdian, David. <u>David Meltzer: A Sketch from Memory and Descriptive Checklist</u>. Berkeley: Oyez, 1965, esp. 3-9.

Enumerative coverage of primary printed sources to 1965.
Superseded by Item 182.

182. _____. "David Meltzer." In his <u>Six Poets of the San Francisco
Renaissance: Portraits and Checklists</u>. Fresno, Calif.:
Giligia Press, 1967, 95-106, esp. 99-106.

Includes works by and about Meltzer into 1966. Enumerative

treatment accompanied by descriptive notes and indications of subject for secondary materials.

MEREDITH, WILLIAM (1919 -)

183. Ludwig, Richard M. "A Checklist of the Writings of William Meredith." Princeton University Library Chronicle 25.1 (Autumn 1963): 79-85.

Reliable, enumerative coverage of primary works through mid-1963.

MERRILL, JAMES (1926 -)

184. Hagstrom, Jack W. C., and George Bixby. "James Merrill: A Bibliographical Checklist." American Book Collector NS 4.6 (November-December 1983): 34-47.

Furnishes a scrupulously thorough list of Merrill's separately published works into 1983, including broadsides, fugitive autobiographical statements and literary notes as well as anthology appearances. Treatment is fully descriptive but excludes periodical publications.

MERWIN, W. S. (1927 -)

185. Quitslund, Jon. "A Checklist of the Writings of William Stanley Merwin." Princeton University Library Chronicle 25.1 (Autumn 1963): 94-104.

Sound treatment of works by Merwin, including translations, into late 1963. Coverage of anthology appearances is selective.

MERTON, THOMAS (1915-1968)

186. Dell'Isola, Frank. "A Bibliography of Thomas Merton." Thought 29 (Winter 1954-1955): 574-596.

Superseded by Item 187.

187. _____. Thomas Merton: A Bibliography. New York: Farrar, Straus and Cudahy, 1956.

Primary coverage superseded by Item 189, except for list of unpublished works. Chronologically arranged record of significant secondary items into 1956 remains useful.

188. Breit, Marquita E. Thomas Merton: A Bibliography. Metuchen, N.J.: Scarecrow Press and the American Theological Library Association, 1974.

Enumeratively records works by and about Merton from 1957 through 1973. Coverage restricted to materials indexed in standard bibliographical tools. Primary section superseded by Item 189. Secondary section remains valuable but is not annotated.

189. Dell'Isola, Frank. Thomas Merton: A Bibliography. Kent, Ohio: Kent State Univ. Press, 1975.

Full account of Merton's published writings through 1973. Separate publications accorded complete descriptions. Publishing history of individual poems handled in a separate section.

MORGAN, ROBERT (1944 -)

190. Wright, Stuart. "Robert Morgan: A Bibliographical Chronicle, 1963-

1981." Bulletin of Bibliography 39.3 (September 1982): 121-
131.

Thorough coverage of primary and secondary printed sources
through 1981. Chronological treatment of works by Morgan
records subsequent printings of individual poems, while
supplementary notes give basic bibliographic data on separately
published works. Items about Morgan not annotated.

MUELLER, LISEL (1925 -)

191. "A Selective Bibliography." Voyages to the Inland Sea 1 (1971):
19-20.

Basic primary checklist into 1970.

NEMEROV, HOWARD (1920 -)

192. Duncan, Bowie. "Howard Nemerov: A Bibliography." In his The
Critical Reception of Howard Nemerov. Metuchen, N.J.:
Scarecrow Press, 1971, 145-211.

Account of printed works by Nemerov and annotated list of
commentary on him into 1970. Primary coverage records
subsequent printings of individual poems. Secondary notes
indicate content of pieces.

193. Wyllie, Diana E. Elizabeth Bishop and Howard Nemerov: A Reference
Guide. Boston: G. K. Hall, 1983.

A thorough enumerative record of primary and secondary printed
sources into 1981. Treatment of works by Nemerov registers
first and subsequent printings of individual items.
Annotations summarizing arguments provided both for Nemerov's
non-fiction prose and for all secondary entries.

NOLL, BINK (1927 -)

194. Towers, A. Robert, Jr. "A Checklist of the Writings of Bink Noll."
Princeton University Library Chronicle 25.1 (Autumn 1963):
114-115.

List of works by Noll into 1963.

O'HARA, FRANK (1926-1966)

195. Smith, Alexander, Jr. Frank O'Hara: A Comprehensive Bibliography.
New York: Garland, 1979. 2d corr. printing, 1980.

Exhaustive coverage of primary materials (including full range
of non-print categories) and thorough but unconventional record
of secondary items into early 1979. Fully descriptive handling
of separately published works, with supplementary biographical
and bibliographical notes--often drawing on unpublished
sources. Lightly annotated account of published commentary is
arranged chronologically, with separate sections each year for
criticism and for creative responses to O'Hara; excludes pieces
entered in standard indexes but provides a list of artworks
featuring O'Hara as subject.

OLSON, CHARLES (1910-1970)

196. Butterick, George. "A Charles Olson Checklist." West Coast Review
2.1 (Spring 1967): 25-31.

Lists secondary sources, including passing references to Olson,
through 1966.

197. _____, and Albert Glover. A Bibliography of Works By Charles
Olson. New York: Phoenix Book Shop, 1967.

Covers primary materials, including non-print items into 1966.

For separately published works provides basic physical description, with supplementary notes for printing history.

198. _____. "A Bibliography of Writings by Charles Olson: Posthumous Publications." Olson: The Journal of the Charles Olson Archives 7 (Spring 1977): 43-60.

Enumerative account of primary materials, including broadsides, ephemerae, and recordings, published from 1970 into early 1977. Notes detail printing history, and reviews of separately issued items are recorded.

199. Charles Olson: A Supplementary Bibliography. Burnaby, B.C.: Simon Fraser University Library, 1980.

Deliberately designed to supplement and update Items 196, 197, and 198, this unannotated checklist provides enumerative treatment of works by and about Olson that were not included in the earlier bibliographies. Primary section lists individual periodical appearances, extending as well to recordings and manuscripts. Secondary section is arranged alphabetically by author within different categories of materials, with non-print and unpublished manuscript items also included. Reliable coverage into the mid-1970s.

200. Groves, Percilla. "Archival Sources for Olson Studies." Line 1 (Spring 1983): 94-102.

An inventory of Olson-related manuscripts and tape recordings held by the Contemporary Literarture Collection of Simon Fraser University Library. Arranged by manuscript group, it records

unpublished materials both by and about Olson. Complements
Item 199.

OPPEN, GEORGE (1908 -)

201. Cuddihy, Michael. "An Oppen Bibliography." Ironwood 5 (1975):
86-87.

202. Gitin, David. "An Oppen Bibliography: Some Amendments." Ironwood
9 (1977): 116.

Together provide an informal treatment of works by and about
Oppen through 1975.

203. Hatlen, Burton, and Julie Courant. "Annotated Chronological
Bibliography of Discussions of George Oppen's Work: Reviews,
Articles, Essays, and Books." In George Oppen: Man and Poet.
Ed. Burton Hatlen. Orono, Me.: National Poetry Foundation,
1981, 463-504.

Includes all significant secondary references. Items heavily
annotated, with frequent quotations from source. Based on and
supplements Item 204.

204. McAleavey, David. "A Bibliography of Discussions of George Oppen's
Work: Reviews, Articles, Essays, and Books." In George Oppen:
Man and Poet. Ed. Burton Hatlen. Orono, Me.: National Poetry
Foundation, 1981, 451-462.

Thorough listing of discussions of Oppen into 1981. Arranged
alphabetically by critic. Not annotated. Supplemented and
complemented by Item 203.

205. _____. "A Bibliography of the Works of George Oppen."
     Paideuma 10.1 (Spring 1981): 155-169.
     Enumerative coverage of primary materials through approximately
     1980. Handling of periodical appearances is unorthodox but
     indicates subsequent publication in collections and notes
     degree of textual variation.

OPPENHEIMER, JOEL (1930 -)

206. Butterick, George F. Joel Oppenheimer: A Checklist of his
     Writings. Storrs: Univ. of Connecticut Library, 1975.
     Enumerative treatment of both primary (printed only) and
     secondary sources, extending to early 1975. Section on
     periodical appearances notes later inclusion in collections but
     does not record all of Oppenheimer's journalistic work.

ORLOVITZ, GIL (1918-1973)

207. Daniels, Guy. "Notes Toward a Bibliography of Gil Orlovitz."
     American Poetry Review 7.6 (November-December 1978): 31-32.
     Brief coverage of primary materials, including recordings,
     tapes, and play productions, through 1976. Periodical
     publication of individual poems not noted.

OWENS, ROCHELLE (1936 -)

208. "Bibliography" for "A Symposium on Rochelle Owens." Margins 23-26
     (1975): 132-133.
     Checklist of works by Owens, including recordings, and
     commentary on her work, into 1975.

PHILLIPS, ROBERT S. (1938 -)

209. Baker, Tom. "Robert Phillips: A Checklist, 1960-1981." Bulletin of Bibliography 38.3 (July-September 1981): 139-149.

Exacting record of printed materials by and about Phillips through 1981. Primary coverage extends to ephemerae and regularly notes subsequent printings of pieces originally published in periodicals. Secondary section is equally thorough.

PLATH, SYLVIA (1932-1963)

210. Homberger, Eric. A Chronological Checklist of the Periodical Publications of Sylvia Plath. Exeter, Eng.: American Arts Documentation Centre, Univ. of Exeter, 1970.

Significantly supplements the primary periodical texts entered in Item 212, especially for juvenalia. Later republication of pieces not indicated.

211. Kinzie, Mary. "An Informal Check List of Criticism." In The Art of Sylvia Plath: A Symposium. Ed. Charles Newman. Bloomington: Indiana Univ. Press; London: Faber and Faber, 1970, 283-304.

Heavily annotated listing of secondary sources through 1967.

212. _____, Daniel Lynn Conrad, and Suzanne D. Kurman. "Bibliography." In The Art of Sylvia Plath: A Symposium. Ed. Charles Newman. Bloomington: Indiana Univ. Press; London: Faber and Faber, 1970, 305-319.

Enumerative record of primary works into 1968. Treatment of periodical publication of poetry includes indication of subsequent appearances.

213.   Northouse, Cameron, and Thomas P. Walsh.   _Sylvia Plath and Anne_
       Sexton: A Reference Guide.   Boston: G. K. Hall, 1974.
       Chronological coverage of works by and about Plath into 1973.
       Primary treatment is strictly enumerative, without any
       connections between periodical and book appearances.
       Annotations in secondary section indicate contents of items.

214.   Cunningham, Stuart.   "Bibliography: Sylvia Plath."   _Hecate_ 1.2
       (July 1975):   95-112.
       Primary treatment concentrates on identifying various
       publications of individual pieces, usefully complementing
       arrangement of earlier work but superseded by Item 215.
       Secondary section unannotated.   The whole marked by minor
       errors and omissions.

215.   Lane, Gary, and Maria Stevens.   _Sylvia Plath: A Bibliography_.
       Metuchen, N.J.:   Scarecrow Press, 1978.
       Thorough record of works by and about Plath into 1977.   Non-
       descriptive primary sections include manuscript and non-print
       materials.   Publication history of individual poems and prose
       pieces traced.   Secondary coverage not annotated.

216.   Lane, Gary.   "Sylvia Plath: A Selective Bibliography of Primary and
       Secondary Materials."   In his _Sylvia Plath: New Views on the_
       Poetry.   Baltimore: Johns Hopkins Univ. Press, 1979, 241-252.
       Though selective, useful for listing of uncollected primary
       materials and of secondary sources through 1978.

POLLAK, FELIX   (1909 -   )

217.   "Selective Checklist." Voyages to the Inland Sea 2 (1972):   28-30.

Sound treatment of works by Pollak, including material

published pseudonymously, into 1972.

REED, ISHMAEL   (1938 -   )

218.   Weixlmann, Joe, Robert Fikes, Jr., and Ishmael Reed. "Mapping Out

the Gumbo Works: An Ishmael Reed Bibliography."   Black

American Literature Forum 12.1 (Spring 1978): 24-29.

Records printed sources by and about Reed into 1977.

Enumerative treatment of primary works notes variant editions

of separately published works but not subsequent publications

of individual items.   Secondary coverage unannotated.

219.   Settle, Elizabeth A., and Thomas A. Settle.   Ishmael Reed: An

Annotated Checklist.   Carson: California State College,

Dominguez Hills, 1977.

Fully incorporated in Item 220.

220.   _____.   Ishmael Reed: A Primary and Secondary Bibliography.

Boston: G. K. Hall, 1982.

Chronological coverage of primary (including non-print) and

secondary materials through 1980 and into 1981.   Index connects

original publication of single works with subsequent appearance

in collections and anthologies.   Annotations carefully

summarize content of both Reed's own non-fiction prose and

critical commentary on him.

REXROTH, KENNETH   (1905-1982)

221. Hartzell, James, and Richard Zumwinkle. Kenneth Rexroth: A
      Checklist of His Published Writings. Los Angeles: Friends of
      the UCLA Library, University of California, Los Angeles, 1967.
      Chronologically organized coverage of primary printed materials
      through 1965. Publication history of individual poems and
      essays briefly noted.

222. Gibson, Morgan. "Rexroth's Books: 1972-79." Ark 14 (1980): 36-
      37.
      An enumerative record of books by Rexroth, intended to
      supplement the bibliography in Gibson's Twayne's United States
      Authors Series volume on Rexroth.

RICH, ADRIENNE   (1929 -)

223. "Bibliography." In Adrienne Rich's Poetry: Texts of the Poems, The
      Poet on Her Work, Reviews and Criticisms. Ed. Barbara Charles-
      worth Gelpi and Albert Gelpi. New York: Norton, 1975, 205-
      207.
      Highly selective list of primary sources. Periodical
      appearances of poems not recorded but account of prose pieces
      is useful.

224. Cooper, Jane Roberta. "Bibliography." In her Reading Adrienne
      Rich: Reviews and Re-Visions, 1951-81. Ann Arbor: Univ. of
      Michigan Press, 1984, 329-365.
      Provides detailed record of Rich's separately published prose
      and thorough listing of secondary materials, with more
      substantive commentary well annotated. Separate publication

and anthology appearances of individual poems not included.
Coverage extends into 1983.

ROETHKE, THEODORE   (1908-1963)

225. McLeod, James Richard.   Theodore Roethke: A Manuscript Checklist.
Kent, Ohio: Kent State Univ. Press, 1971.

Provides a detailed inventory of Roethke's manuscripts held in
public institutions. Arranged by separate books, with
supplementary sections for unpublished works and letters.
Treatment allows identification and location of manuscript
versions of individual poems and prose pieces.

226. _____. Theodore Roethke: A Bibliography. Kent, Ohio: Kent
State Univ. Press, 1973.

Thorough coverage of primary and secondary sources, including
non-print items, into 1972. Handling of Roethke's separate
publications is fully descriptive, with supplementary notes
indicating both printing history of individual pieces and any
variants. Record of commentary on Roethke is very detailed for
biographical materials (including notices in local and college
newspapers) but somewhat selective for critical studies and
reviews. Secondary section not annotated.

227. Moul, Keith R. Theodore Roethke's Career: An Annotated Bibliogra-
aphy. Boston: G. K. Hall, 1977.

Enumerative account of printed materials by and about Roethke.
Primary coverage provides minimal information, adding little to
Item 226. Chronologically organized secondary section includes

local reviews not in Item 226 and extends coverage through 1973. It is also fully annotated.

ROSELIEP, RAYMOND (1917 -)

228. "Selected Bibliography." Voyages to the Inland Sea 4 (1974): 74-79.

Sound coverage of primary and secondary materials, including recordings, into 1973.

RUMAKER, MICHAEL (1932 -)

229. Butterick, George. "Michael Rumaker: A Checklist." Athanor 6 (Spring 1975): 45-49.

Checklist of primary texts, through 1974.

SEBENTHALL, R. E. (1917 -)

230. "Bibliography." In Voyages to the Inland Sea 3 (1973): 31-32.

Primary and secondary checklist, including periodical and anthology appearances, into 1972.

SEXTON, ANNE (1928-1974)

231. Northouse, Cameron, and Thomas P. Walsh. Sylvia Plath and Anne Sexton: A Reference Guide. Boston: G. K. Hall, 1974.

Chronological lists of works by and about Sexton through 1971. Primary coverage does not indicate subsequent publication of poems originally printed in magazines. Secondary section has content notes.

SIMIC, CHARLES (1938 -)

232. "Charles Simic: Bibliography." Manassas Review 1.2 (Winter 1978): 63-67.

Checklist of printed sources by and about Simic into 1977. Treatment of periodical appearances of poems specifies only the names of magazines containing items. Coverage of reviews of Simic's separately published volumes is thorough.

233. Seluzicki, Charles. "Charles Simic: A Bibliographical Checklist." American Book Collector NS 3.4 (July/August 1982): 34-39.

Provides brief descriptions of first editions of separately published works by Simic, or with contributions from him, through 1981.

SIMPSON, LOUIS (1923 -)

234. Roberson, William H. Louis Simpson: A Reference Guide. Boston: G. K. Hall, 1980.

Comprehensively covers works both by and about Simpson through 1979. Primary section arranged chronologically within types of publications (e.g., Books, Poems in Periodicals, Poems in Books) with treatment strictly enumerative, though contents of books are listed and index allows tracing of different appearances of individual pieces. Secondary coverage is exceptionally thorough, with entries well annotated.

SLOTE, BERNICE

235. Pigaga, Thom. "Bernice Slote: A Check List of Published Writings." Prairie Schooner 55.1-2 (Spring/Summer 1981): 114-119.

Fully records poems published in periodicals over the period 1945-1959.

SMITH, DAVE   (1942 -)

236. Weigl, Bruce. "Bibliography." In his The Giver of Morning: On the
        Poetry of Dave Smith. Birmingham, Ala.: Thunder City Press,
        1982, [89-92].

        Provides enumerative treatment of primary and secondary
        publications into 1981. Appearances of Smith's essays in
        anthologies, books, and periodicals are noted, but similar
        coverage of individual poems is absent.

SNODGRASS, W. D.   (1926 -)

237. White, William. W. D. Snodgrass: A Bibliography. Detroit: Wayne
        State Univ. Library, 1960.

        Descriptive account of primary publications and unannotated
        list of secondary sources, into 1960.   Regularly notes
        subsequent appearances of poems originally printed in
        periodicals.

SNYDER, GARY   (1930 -)

238. Kherdian, David. A Biographical Sketch and Descriptive Checklist of
        Gary Snyder. Berkeley: Oyez, 1965.

        Bibliographical information fully incorporated in Item 239.

239. _____. "Gary Snyder." In his Six Poets of the San Francisco
        Renaissance: Portraits and Checklists. Fresno, Calif.:
        Giligia Press, 1967, 47-70, esp. 55-70.

        Lists materials by and about Snyder to 1966. Entries for books
        accompanied by informal descriptive notes.

240. Norton, David. "Gary Snyder: A Checklist." Schist 2 (Summer

1974): 58-66.

Restricted to primary sources, with coverage extending into early 1974.

241. McNeil, Katherine. Gary Snyder: A Bibliography. New York: Phoenix Bookshop, 1983.

Exhaustive account of primary materials, including non-print and ephemeral items through 1976 only. Books given basic physical description, supplemented by notes on other relevant bibliographical facts. Index allows tracing printing history of individual poems. Selective, unannotated section of secondary references is the most thorough available.

SPICER, JACK (1925-1965)

242. Dorbin, Sanford. "A Checklist of the Published Writings of Jack Spicer." California Librarian 31.4 (October 1970): 251-261.

Account of works by Spicer, including recordings, through 1970. Informal notes furnish some descriptive information about separate publications. Reprintings of individual poems regularly registered.

243. Blaser, Robin. "Bibliography of the First Editions." In The Collected Books of Jack Spicer. Ed. Robin Blaser. Los Angeles: Black Sparrow Press, 1975, 381-382.

Treats Spicer's separate publications into 1974. Principal interest lies with informal notes accompanying enumerative entries.

244. Dorbin, Sandy. "Spicer Bibliography: An Interim Report." _Schist_ 4/5 (1976-1978): 180-187.

    Supplements and updates the coverage of primary materials provided in Item 242, but excludes periodical appearances. Adds an unannotated list of writings about Spicer into 1977.

STAFFORD, WILLIAM (1914 -)

245. McMillan, Samuel H. "On William Stafford and His Poems: A Selected Bibliography." _Tennessee Poetry Journal_ 2.3 (Spring 1969): 21-22.

    Unannotated list of secondary sources into 1968, principally from major journals but with some little magazine references.

246. Holdin, Jonathan. "Bibliography." In his _The Mark to Turn: A Reading of William Stafford's Poetry_. Lawrence: Univ. Press of Kansas, 1976, 85-87.

    Selected works by and about Stafford into 1975. Of value only in absence of other bibliographical work.

TAGGART, JOHN (1942 -)

247. "Bibliography: John Taggart." _Stations_ 3-4 (1976): 129-131.

    Enumerative presentation of poetry and prose by Taggart into 1975, including sound treatment of anthology and magazine appearances. Reviews of his work also listed.

248. "Partial Bibliography: JT." _Paper Air_ 2.1 (1979): 72.

    Selective checklist of primary works, including non-print material.

TRUDELL, DENNIS (1935 -)

249. "Dennis Trudell: A Bibliography." Voyages to the Inland Sea 5

(1975): 48-50.

Lists works by Trudell into 1975.

TURCO, LEWIS (1934 -)

250. Lewis Turco: A Bibliography of His Works and of Criticism of Them.

Potsdam, N.Y.: F. W. Crumb Memorial Library, State Univ.

College, 1969.

Records printed works by and about Turco into 1969. Carefully

notes magazine and anthology publication of individual poems

later collected.

WAGONER, DAVID (1926 -)

251. "Bibliography and Checklist of Criticisms" in "David Wagoner Issue."

Slackwater Review (1981): 124-127.

Primary coverage limited to separately published works into

1981; treatment of secondary items is selective.

WHALEN, PHILIP (1923 -)

252. Kherdian, David. "Philip Whalen." In his Six Poets of the San

Francisco Renaissance: Portraits and Checklists. Fresno,

Calif: Giligia Press, 1967, 73-92, esp. 77-92.

Sound coverage of both primary (including non-print and

ephemeral items) and secondary sources through 1966.

Enumerative approach with supplementary notes.

WHITTEMORE, REED (1919 -)

253. "(Edward) Reed Whittemore (Jr)." Voyages 3.3-4 (Spring 1979): 10-

11.

An abbreviated biography and primary checklist providing some useful bibliographical information.

WIENERS, JOHN (1934 -)

254. Butterick, George F. "John Wieners: A Checklist." *Athanor* 3 (Summer-Fall 1973): 53-63.

Thorough record of primary texts through 1971, with unannotated list of pertinent secondary sources. Treatment of works by Wieners is enumerative but informal notes provide additional bibliographical information.

WILBUR, RICHARD (1921 -)

255. Field, John P. *Richard Wilbur: A Bibliographical Checklist.* Kent, Ohio: Kent State Univ. Press, 1971.

Provides thorough record of primary (including manuscripts and non-print) and secondary sources through 1969. Treatment of books by Wilbur is enumerative but notes sketch printing histories. Republication of individual poems traced in separate section. Secondary entries not annotated.

256. Dinneen, Marcia B. "Richard Wilbur: A Bibliography of Secondary Sources." *Bulletin of Bibliography* 37.1 (January-March 1980): 16-22.

Continues the secondary coverage of Item 255 into 1978, providing annotations that summarize content of each item. Restricted to materials listed in standard indexes and excludes many short reviews.

WILLIAMS, JONATHAN (1929 -)

257. [Greene, Jonathan]. "Titles By Jonathan Williams." Truck 21
    (1979): n. pag.

    Checklist of books and broadsides by Williams, including
    volumes of photography and titles edited.

WOODS, JOHN (1926 -)

258. "Selected Bibliography." Voyages to the Inland Sea 2 (1972): 79.

    Primary coverage, including recordings but excluding periodical
    appearances, into 1972.

WRIGHT, CHARLES (1935 -)

259. Wright, Stuart. "Charles Wright: A Bibliographic Chronicle, 1963-
    1985." Bulletin of Bibliography 43.1 (March 1986):
    [forthcoming].

    Furnishes a scrupulously thorough, enumerative treatment of
    Wright's printed works into 1985, with references to books,
    broadsides, and periodical appearances arranged in a single
    chronological sequence. Republication of individual poems in
    both Wright's own collections and in anthologies is noted, so
    that the publishing history of specific pieces can be easily
    traced.

WRIGHT, JAMES (1927-1980)

260. McMaster, Belle M. "James Arlington Wright: A Checklist."
    Bulletin of Bibliography and Magazine Notes 31.2 (April-June
    1974): 71-82, 88.

    Exacting coverage of primary materials, including records and
    tapes but excluding interviews, through 1973. Scrupulously

registers later publications of poems and translations originally printed in periodicals, with indication when revision of
text occurred. Brief supplementary notes throughout furnish
other essential bibliographic information.

261. Cuddihy, Michael. "Bibliography." Ironwood 10 (1977): 156-165.
Checklist of printed works by and about Wright into 1976.
Primary coverage updates Item 260, but for period through 1973
is not as reliable or complete. Account of secondary items is
not exhaustive but includes numerous little magazine
references.

262. "Selected Bibliography." In The Pure Clear Word: Essays on the
Poetry of James Wright. Ed. Dave Smith. Urbana: Univ. of
Illinois Press, 1982, 247-257.
Updates and expands the primary and secondary coverage of Item
261, but repeats the earlier checklist's errors and omissions.
Valuable for more current citations, especially of criticism of
Wright.

ZUKOFSKY, LOUIS (1904-1978)

263. Zukofsky, Celia. A Bibliography of Louis Zukofsky. Los Angeles:
Black Sparrow Press, 1969.
Records primary materials, including taped readings, through
1968. Enumerative treatment of separate publications,
supplemented by notes covering basic production information.
Absence of content notes makes impossible the tracing of
printing histories of individual poems. Includes chronological
account of manuscripts.

264. Booth, Marcella. A Catalogue of the Louis Zukofsky Manuscript
     Collection. Austin: Humanities Research Center, Univ. of
     Texas at Austin, 1975.

     Provides detailed content analysis and physical description of
     Zukofsky manuscripts at the University of Texas–Austin. Body
     of catalog preceded by brief enumerative account of his books
     and pamphlets, with listing of contents of each.

265. Zukofsky, Celia. "Year by Year Bibliography of Louis Zukofsky."
     Paideuma 7.3 (Winter 1978): 603–610.

     Updates through 1978 the chronological account of Zukofsky's
     manuscripts in Item 263.

266. Terrell, Carroll F. "A Bibliography of Works about Louis Zukofsky
     with Extended Commentary." In his Louis Zukofsky: Man and
     Poet. Orono, Me.: National Poetry Foundation, 1979, 401–438.

     Chronologically arranged coverage of significant commentary on
     Zukofsky from 1945 into 1978. Extensive annotations and
     quotations accompany most items.

267. Zukofsky, Celia. "Year by Year Bibliography of Louis Zukofsky." In
     Louis Zukofsky: Man and Poet. Ed. Carrol F. Terrell. Orono,
     Me.: National Poetry Foundation, 1979, 385–392.

     Reprints Item 265.